Amazon Echo User Guide

*Comprehensive Guide to Getting The Most
out of Amazon Echo*

Simon Bedford

Table of Contents

Sample Connection Model for your Color Expert Blueprint Model

How to Build Custom Skills

Working with the Alexa Skills Kit

Alexa Fund Investments

Simple Tricks You Can Try with Your Amazon Echo

Tips And Tricks For Using Amazon Echo At The Highest Potential

Shop on Amazon

How to Set Up Automatic Purchases on Your Amazon Echo

How to Setup Voice Purchasing

Voice Purchasing Requirements

Going About Digital Music Purchases on Alexa

Going About Physical Product Purchases on Alexa

How to reorder Prime-Eligible Items with Alexa

Enjoy Amazon Prime Music

How to Buy Digital Music with Alexa

What to Do When You Place an Accidental Order

What to Expect When Shopping With Alexa: Some Alexa Shopping Responses to Look Out For

When you attempt to place an order without Prime membership

When you attempt to make an order but Alexa notices a problem with the 1-click billing address on your Amazon account

How to Upload Offline Music to Your Amazon Music Library and Play the Music on Your Echo Device

Load your own music to the Echo!

Enjoy New Prime Stations

Listen to iHeart Radio Music

Enjoy Your Favorite Pandora Radio Stations

Receive Accurate Weather Reports

Access Information Instantly

Get Accurate Traffic Updates Any Time

Create and Manage Your Shopping List with Ease

Listening to Music On Amazon Echo

Working with alarms

You Will Love Home Automation Services

How To Connect LIFX Bulbs To The Echo And Use Alexa To Control Them

Access Wikipedia Articles through Voice command

Use Amazon from Different Accounts

Introduction

Today, more and more people are seeking devices that will be highly convenient and require minimal input to work effectively. In addition to this convenience, there is a need to have a device that offers quick solutions. This is the origin of the Amazon Echo.

So what is Amazon Echo?

Amazon Echo is a 9.75-inch voice command, cylinder-like speaker. It has a 7-piece microphone-arrangement speaker that includes a woofer and a remote control. The device runs on Amazon web services, and it is set from the factory to listen to all speech waiting for the wake word to be spoken. For it to work, it has to be connected to a Wi-Fi internet network.

So what can it do?

Amazon echo can:

✓ **Provide answers to questions.** For instance, it can give you information about things in your Google calendar, general questions that you need answers for, and any question you would like to ask for fun.

✓ **Play music. You can play music from your Amazon** music account and from streaming services like iTunes, Spotify, and Pandora radio. You can also use it to play music from other devices via Bluetooth.

✓ **Control smart** devices in your home that are connected to it.

✓   Offer reliable news and weather services from several sources, such as local radio stations.

✓   Support voice controlled alarms, shopping lists, to-do-lists, timers, and so many services that can help you stay organized.

✓   Can give you access to Wikipedia articles on command.

Its functionality improves over time since it is connected to the Cloud and Amazon adds new features to it all the time.

With these amazing capabilities, it is now time to get started with Amazon Echo. So where do you start? Let's learn that in the next chapter.

Getting Started with Your Amazon Echo

Getting to Know the Features of Echo

Action Button

Press down on the Action button to turn off the alarm and timer
Select this button to wake Echo up

Microphone Button

Press this button to shut off the microphone
The light ring turns red indicating it is off
Re-press the button and it is turned back on

Light Ring

The Light Ring Tells you what Echo is doing

Look at the light ring and it will inform you what action Echo is
performing (For Example, if the light ring is blue this means Echo is
ready to Receive Requests)

Volume Ring

Turn the volume dial clockwise to increase the volume
Turn the dial counterclockwise to decrease the volume
The Light ring fills in as the volume increases
The light ring will decrease as the volume decreases

Where to put Your Echo

Put the echo in a central location – this is where it works best – at
least 8 inches from any walls.
Kitchen counter
Bedroom nightstand

End table in your living room

Try Some Things with your Echo: *News, Weather and Traffic Commands:*
News:
"Alexa, play NPR."

Weather commands:
"Alexa, what's the weather?"

"Alexa, will it rain tomorrow?"

Traffic commands:

"Alexa, how is my commute looking?"

Alarm and Timer Commands:

Alarm:

"Alexa, will you set the alarm for 7 a.m."

Timer:

"Alexa, configure the timer for 45 minutes."

"Alexa, snooze."

Calendar Commands:
"Alexa, what is on my calendar for tomorrow?"

"Alexa, when is my next meeting?"

To-Do Lists and Shopping Lists Commands

To-Do Lists:

"Alexa, add milk to my shopping list

Shopping Lists

"Alexa, I have to make a birthday cake."

"Alexa, tell me about the to-do list?"

Shop on Amazon

Order items from Amazon.com Commands:

"Alexa, re-order laundry detergent."

"Alexa, buy more toothpaste."

Questions and Answers Commands

"Alexa, I need to hear a joke."

"Alexa, what is the height of the Empire State building?"

"Alexa, how many ounces are in a cup?"

"Alexa, what's the definition of serendipity?"

"Alexa, when is Mother's Day?"

"Alexa, Wikipedia: Abraham Lincoln."

"Alexa, what is the time in Moscow?"

Prime Music commands:
(You can play music from the Prime catalog for free.)
"Alexa, play some Prime Music."

"Alexa, play some relaxing music."

"Alexa, play my Jimi Hendrix station."

"Alexa, add this to my library."

Sports commands:

"Alexa, did DC United win?"

"Alexa, what is the score of the Cubs game?"

"Alexa, when do the San Francisco 49ers play again??"

The internet and mobile devices are altering the way people communicate and view convenience. As it stands, leading mobile companies including Apple, Google and Microsoft all have voice activated platforms in the form of 'assistants' to help make life easier for users. Amazon now has its very own virtual assistant, known as Alexa, the native assistance present in the Amazon Echo.

The Amazon Echo is a device that has its focus on the future, as it brings to the fore voice control and a type of 'robot' in the home. Using web intelligence, this device is able to transform the way that one relates to the home, particularly in smart functionalities.

Note: By virtue of being a web-enabled device, you must have Wi-Fi connectivity in order to use your Amazon Echo.

There is one special attribute that enables the Amazon Echo to stand out significantly from the competition, and that is the fact that it is entirely hands free. With your mobile device, you need to use a button to access the assistant. This hand-free attribute is what ensures that the Echo has a firm place in the future.

When you receive your Amazon Echo, it usually is packaged in a minimalist style black box. Inside the box, you will see the Echo, which is black in color and cylindrical in shape. It is about the same height as two cans of soup, which is 9.75 inches. Its diameter is 3.27 inches.

As it is primarily a speaker, inside the Amazon Echo, you will find a 2.5-inch woofer, a 2.0-inch tweeter, 7 microphones, and at the very top, the light ring and volume ring adjustment. The light ring will light up in different colors depending on the command that has been given once the wake word is given. The volume ring can be adjusted by turning it clockwise for volume increase and in the opposite direction to reduce the volume.

At the top of your Echo, you will notice that there are two buttons. The symbol on one button is a microphone; this button will effectively switch off the microphone. The other button is for numerous actions. These buttons can be used for switching things off, but they do not switch anything on.

Note: When ordering your Amazon Echo, you should request that the remote control be included as part of your order. It is worth noting that your Amazon Echo needs to be plugged into an electrical outlet at all times as it does not operate on battery power. This means that you should locate it somewhere accessible to you and you won't need to move it too much. Although it can pick up your voice from quite a distance, you may prefer having it close by so that you can see the light ring and its reactions to your voice commands.

Now that you have the Amazon Echo, you can ensure that you get the most out of it by starting off on the right foot. Therefore, to get started with the use of your Amazon Echo, you can either:

Say the wake word Alexa, or any other wake word that you have chosen.

Press the action button, which is at the top of the Amazon Echo.

Press and hold the Amazon's Echo remote control talk button.

You can ask your device a question, for instance, what the weather is in a certain area. Give it a command like what you want on your shopping list, what you want to be reminded on a certain day or at a certain time. You can also command the device to play you a particular song. All these requests or commands are processed in the Cloud, and this is what allows the device to do just what you ask.

Amazon Echo is capable of exchanging information with third party services in order to fulfill your commands in their entirety. This is what makes the Amazon Echo such an excellent device to get what you require in as little time as possible.

The Amazon Echo also comes with integrated Bluetooth services, and this allows it to access information. For example, it can access music from other Bluetooth-enabled devices around it. You do not need to transfer music from your smart device to your Echo since you can always access it and play your favorite hits through the Echo.

An excellent advantage of using the Amazon Echo is that its services are improving over time; the voice services, for instance, get better as you continue using the device. Its speed and accuracy improve with time as well. Amazon is constantly looking out for ways to make this device better for its users. Therefore, if you realize that you do not like something about the device, the providers are always waiting for feedback in order to make things better for all the users.

Why Should You Own An Amazon Echo?

Amazon Echo has been likened to a very useful robot speaker that can do so much for you, for instance, set your alarms, play your favorite music, make a shopping list for you, and even look up answers for the questions you ask by just talking to it. It is very convenient for use especially at home, and so many users have called it a smart home device. So what are some of the things that the device can offer that are just outstanding?

✓ **It offers great convenience to the user**

Amazon Echo offers so much convenience to its users. You do not need to do everything for yourself; for instance, play music, check out certain information on your laptop, control your home devices, set up reminders and alarms and so much more; as these are things that you can command the device to do for you.

It is not hard at all to get information on your computer or smartphone, but with Echo, you can do this as well as working on something else at the same time. If your hands are full, you will still get the information and help that you are looking for at that time. This is the kind of convenience you enjoy with Alexa.

If you are working on an urgent project or are busy doing house chores, you will not miss out on breaking news and this does not mean that you will take a break from what you are doing. This is the perfect device to help you multitask and achieve more in a short period of time.

Let your device help you finish a task on time. It can provide accurate information to help you finish a task you are working on. If, for instance, you need to know the distance between San Francisco and

Boston for your project, you do not need to take a break to check it out. Just ask your Echo.

✓ **The Alexa App**

Amazon app also comes with an Alexa Mobile app for Android users, iOS and Amazon Fire users. Through this app, you can track down all your activities with the Echo. You are also able to change the settings of your device in order to enjoy more services through it.

The app works using a web browser, and through it, you can train your Echo in various ways. You can use it to conveniently queue up the music that you would like to listen to, as well as check the history of your activities. Furthermore, you can use the app to help build up speech recognition making it easier for you to communicate with your Echo.

All your to-do-lists, shopping lists, questions, and answers can be accessed through this app, and this means that if you need a record of the same, you can always access it with ease. It is also possible to control these lists using the app, particularly if you want to take items off the list or access the list when you are going grocery shopping. This app adds so much value to the device. It helps you set your device personalized as you wish, as well as, trace back your Amazon Echo's activities.

✓ **Entertainment**

Amazon Echo is a great entertainment device. Its quality speakers will always play your favorite music at your command. Connect the speakers to your other devices to play your music via Bluetooth. The speakers are loud enough, clear and of great quality; therefore, you will always enjoy quality entertainment from it.

✓ **Smart**

You can always get what you need at a given time through your Amazon Echo. If you are bored, the device will detect your mood and play the kind of music that will bring you back to the right mood. If you are happy, it will know and so the kind of music it will select for you is one that will match your current mood.

✓ **Cloud Integration**

Amazon Echo is always getting smarter as it is connected to the cloud and this means that you can expect a lot more from your device as the technology advances. Amazon is always adding features to the Echo to improve the way it serves its users. You do not want to miss this.

✓ **Fun**

Using Amazon Echo is so much fun. There is a lot that you can do with your device for fun, like using it as an intercom in the house to send messages to your family. You can also use it to check out where someone is in the house instead of checking it out yourself. It can find your phone if you have misplaced it! This is a device that you will enjoy so much to have in your home.

✓ **Automated Shopping**

Amazon Echo is a device that will conduct commerce on your behalf. Just let it know what you want to buy and the device will buy it for you. This is the kind of convenience Echo users are enjoying these days, as they do not have to really shop for what they need.

✓ **Amazon Echo Integration**

You can set up your Echo to be of even more use to you by ensuring that you integrate it with a range of devices. This cuts out your need to depend on too many platforms, and simply makes your life and the management of all that you do so much easier. All these are possible due to the capability of the Echo to operate in a cloud; which means that large amounts of information can be made accessible without there being any negative effect on the functionality of the device.

✓   **Home Integration**

As a tool that can significantly affect the operations of the home, integrating the echo to relevant household devices is relatively simple. Take for example Philip Hue lighting. By integrating the lighting with your Echo, you will be able to control its functions with your voice. This becomes possible with voice commands.

All you need to do is ask Alexa to do a search of your home to find any home control devices. If these devices are on the same Wi-Fi network, finding them will be quite easy. After they have been found and identified, you will need to refer to your Alexa app. Once you see your preferred devices, in this case, Philip Hue, then you can select that option. This will then integrate the device with Alexa. From this juncture, it becomes easy to give Alexa commands so that she is able to control the lighting. Let's take a closer look at this:

Use It as a Controller for Your Other Devices

Amazon Echo can be connected to your other smart devices and appliances at home for you to be able to control them from one central place with ease. If you are baking, for instance, command it to set your oven to a particular temperature and it will be done. This is meant to make things a lot easier for you, and since it only requires a voice command, you can do so much at once, and achieve a lot without necessarily doing it yourself.

Use It as Your Weather Reporter

With Amazon Echo at home, you do not need to keep watching TV or listen to Radio in order to know how the weather will be, or how the weather is in a certain location. This device can report to you immediately with only one command. It means that you can always stay informed about weather patterns without necessarily getting involved, which is much better especially for a busy person.

Are you planning a trip in a hurry? This will be a very useful device as it can spare you so much time of checking out how the weather patterns will be like in your destination. Every information you get through the Echo is accurate and reliable.

It can also give you the expected weather of a particular place in a few days to come for proper planning.

Use It as Your Reliable Dispatcher

Use your Amazon Echo to get accurate information pertaining to any service that you could be interested in. If you are planning a trip, you can access information pertaining to the available flights to your destination and what their departure time is. If you want to use a bus, you can get information pertaining to the available bus and the right time to board.

The Echo is a communication device that receives and sends accurate messages, tracking down services you may be interested in to help you out and make things much easier for you.

It is integrated with only a few services from the factory, but you can open up the API to access more services and make your operations much easier with your device as your ultimate dispatcher. The device can use the information to give you the best options to choose from using the information it has about you, for instance, your address.

It Offers You Localized Information

As the Amazon Echo is able to get information from Yelp, you can use it to find out details about the shops that are in your area, as well as any good eateries and other business services and products that you may be interested in. With this integration, the wealth of information available is excellent as you can easily find out what times a business opens and closes, as well as get specific details including phone numbers, the current ratings, and direct links to reviews on Yelp.

To get this information, all you need to do is ask Alexa questions link, 'Alexa, what are the operating hours for a nearby Chinese Restaurant?' and you will get your answer. To enable this skill, you need to use your Alexa app and input your address within settings.

Note: The Amazon Echo is definitely not the first device to be able to do all this but it uses the current technology, which means that it is the best device for this, so far. It only requires software to support it and once it is connected to an internet source, be assured that your life will be much easier than it has been.

✓ **IFTTT Integration**

The more you use Alexa, the more you will need to automate certain functions, especially those that you repeat on a regular basis. If This Then That (IFTTT) is a cloud service that is available for free on the web that is able to do this with ease, by it creating a special recipe.

The integration of Amazon Echo with IFTTT means that automation is easier, and this in turn can be linked to your calendar or things to do list.

To do the integration, you will need to create an IFTTT account, and then go online to find the page for the Alexa channel. Once you find it, you should select the option to connect. After this on your mobile device, you need to find the reminders channel, and select the option to connect. Now you can install the IFTTT for your device, whether it be an Android device or iOS. You will see an option entitled Amazon Alexa, and at this option, you will create your own recipe, simple by choosing it.

Then you will see a list that is referred to as a trigger list. Here, you should add the item that you want to be automated, and then select the option to create a list. These items will help you save time as you create your customized spoken to-do lists.

Some of the most popular Alexa recipes include sending yourself an email of your shopping list when you request Alexa to inform you what is available on your shopping list. You could also add your Alexa to dos to Evernote. Request to receive an iOS notification the moment that you add something to your Alexa To Do list.

As it is, the Amazon Echo with IFTTT is able to connect with Google Drive and Gmail, as well as with Microsoft OneNote and iOS. The other services include Toddled and To do list.

There are more recipes that have been created to help make life more convenient and simple, one of which allows for sending brief SMS messages. To use this, you need to input the cell phone number of the receiver including the country code, and then it will send the message to the shopping list. For Alexa to interpret what you want to add correctly, you should provide her with a direct command, such as "Alexa, add this to my shopping list," and it will become a text message, ready to be forwarded. This recipe is brilliant, though it is limited to Android phones.

Looking out for newer integrations that are being developed is essential, as these will help with the ease of use of Amazon Echo.

Note: We will discuss more on how to achieve each of the capabilities mentioned in this chapter as we go on with the book. This chapter was simply designed to help you get a glimpse of what it is you can achieve with this device. If you are excited to get started, head to the next chapter to learn how to set up the Echo.

Buying and Setting Up your Amazon Echo

Detailed Instructions for Setting up Amazon Echo

1) Download the Alexa app and sign in

The Alexa app will be free of charge for Fire OS, Android, and iOS. Phone and Tablet requirements:

A) Fire OS 2.0 or higher

B) Android 4.0 or higher

C) iOS 7.0 or higher

Download the "Alexa" app by opening the app store on your mobile device and then search for "Alexa app." Or enter one of the following apps on your computer browser search menu:

Amazon app store

Google

Apple App Store

(Kindle Fire 1st and 2nd Generation tablets don't support the Alexa app)

2) Power on Echo

Plug Echo into the supplied power adapter then into a power outlet

Light ring on Echo turns green then orange

Echo communicates with you

3) Connect Echo to Wi-Fi Network

Note: (Echo links to double-band Wi-Fi (2.4 GHz / 5 GHz) networks using the 802.11a / b / g / n standard. Echo will not connect to these network types:

Ad-hoc (or peer-to-peer) networks or Mobile hotspots

1) In the Alexa app, click your left navigation then choose Settings.

2) Pick your device then select Update Wi-Fi or if you are using a new device then select Setup a new device.

3) On the echo device press and hold "Action" button for five seconds until the light ring turns to orange. Now your mobile device is connected to Echo. Available Wi-Fi networks will be listed in your app.

Note: The Alexa app may ask you to connect your device manually to the Echo device through the Wi-Fi settings.

4) Select your Wi-Fi network and enter your network password when you are prompted. If you are unable to see your network, scroll down to "Add a Network" (this is for hidden networks) or select "Rescan."

5) Select "Connect" Your device will connect to the Wi-Fi network, and you will receive a confirmation message indicating you are connected. Alexa is ready to go!

Troubleshooting Wi-Fi that won't connect

What these different colored LED lights mean:

Solid white light: Your Echo device is attached to the Wi-Fi network.

Solid orange light: Your Echo device is not connected to your Wi-Fi network.

Blinking orange light: Your Echo device is connected to your Wi-Fi network, but can't access the Alexa Voice Service.

Try to connect again to the Wi-Fi Network

You will need to know the network password. If there is a lock icon displaying then, you need to enter the network password (This is not your Amazon account password).

You can try and connect other devices (tablets, mobile phones) to your network to test connectivity. If no other devices connect, there may be problems with your Wi-Fi network. Contact your Internet Service Provider, network administrator, or the person who set up your network for help.

Update the firmware for your router or modem.

Did you save your Wi-Fi password to Amazon?

If you recently changed the password, then enter your new Wi-Fi password to connect to the network again

Reduce Wi-Fi Traffic

You may have too many devices connected to your network which will result in poor system performance.

Shut off any devices you're not using. You will free up bandwidth on the network.

Move your device closer to the modem if it is in a different room, or if an object or wall is blocking it.

You need to make sure your device is away from sources that could cause interference (baby monitors or microwave ovens).

Restart your modem and router to resolve many Wi-Fi issues:

Turn off your modem and router then wait 30 seconds.

Turn on your modem and then wait for it to restart.

After you turn on your modem, then turn on your router and wait for it to reset.

While you're waiting for your network hardware to reset, unplug your Echo device from its power adapter. You should wait for three seconds then plug it in again.

Once you restart your Echo device and network hardware, you should try and reconnect to your Wi-Fi network.

If all these steps fail to re-connect your Echo to your Wi-Fi network, then try resetting your Echo:

Use a paper clip or similar tool and use it to press down on the reset button for five seconds. (The Echo reset button is located at the base of your device.) The light ring on your Echo device will turn orange, and then blue.

Wait for the light ring to turn off and then on again. The light ring will turn orange, and your Echo device will go into set-up mode.

Open the Alexa app to link your device to a Wi-Fi network and register it to your Amazon account.

With all the amazing things that Amazon Echo can do for you, it is time to get yourself one. Visit Amazon official website and request for an invitation. Once your invitation is accepted, you will be ready to enjoy its amazing services.

Amazon Echo is always ready for use; so once you buy it, you only need to go through a small set-up process to start giving it commands and receiving feedback.

Amazon Echo's Hardware

From the outside, Amazon Echo is a metallic cylinder that is perforated on most of its outer surface in order to let audio out. Its sound cannot be compared to its small size because it is very powerful, and the quality of its sound is great. It is a very reliable and durable device, and one can be rest assured that it would provide good service for a very long time.

As earlier mentioned, at the top of your Echo are two buttons; the action button and the other one is for activating your microphone for input. Use the action button to turn off alarms, reminders, timers, and to wake the device if you do not want to use the voice command.

If you prefer physical audio control instead of using the voice command, you can always count on its high quality remote control, which comes with the Echo. The remote control comes with all the audio media controls that you'll need to use, and two AAA batteries.

From the manufacturer, your device will come with a power adapter and a remote control. Before you start the set-up process, get a good central location for your device. There are so many places where you can have it in your home; for instance, on your kitchen countertop, in your living room, in your bedroom, and in any other central place that you feel you can be able to use it effectively even when you are in other rooms in the house.

How To Set It Up

Plug in the device into a power source. Connect the power adapter to the device and then to the power outlet socket. Your Echo will illuminate a blue light then an orange light and then greet you. This means that it is ready to work. It has to stay connected to the power source as long as you are using it since it does not have an internal battery.

Insert the batteries provided into the remote control. The remote control and the Echo will connect automatically once the batteries have been inserted. If that does not happen, you will have to pair them up in the Amazon Echo app on your mobile device through the settings.

Download the Alexa app to your smart phone if you do not have it. If you already have it, access it and connect your device to a Wi-Fi network. This app will also help you a lot to review your requests, manage your music and lists, and access the settings in order to personalize your device as much as you want. Once you access the app, connect your device to Wi-Fi and you will be good to go.

*In order to enjoy the above and many more services from your Alexa, set it up. You need a fast Wi-Fi connection in order to use it effectively. The action button will always get you started; long press it for a few seconds until the light changes to orange. Set up your Amazon Echo app on your phone and start using your device.

As long as it is connected to the internet, you can start talking to your device. Remember to always use the wake word Alexa to alert it to receive a command. The wake word Alexa is set by default at the factory, but you can always change it through the app settings.

Once you start using your device, you will slowly realize how much you can achieve through it. You can always check out how much you have done on your device as well, through the history feature in the app settings. Click on each entry in order to get the history of your commands in detail. This way, you are able to check whether the device really got your message correctly or not. Be assured that Amazon Echo is very accurate when it comes to receiving commands and much of what you command is recorded accurately.

Using the Alexa App

To get the most out of your Echo, you will find that you need to make considerable use of the Alexa App. After you have downloaded the app and selected it, you will be directed to the apps Home Screen. Here, it will be possible to review a timeline, which indicates all your recent activities with the amazon Echo.

You can choose from several options. If you choose home, you will find information of your activity and you are able to select to get deeper information. Choosing the To-Do List or Shopping List options will allow you to manage the lists that you have already created using Alexa. You will also be able to add items to the list, which Alexa can update you on later.

There is an option called Now Playing, which lets you see how your music has been queued up, which albums you have lined app, and your player history. With the app, you can look up playlists as well as listen to radio stations.

The option for Alarm allows you to control your alarm settings, and should you need to, selecting off will switch off the alarm until it is reactivated. The same appliers for the Timer option.

You are also able to manage and change the settings on your device, as well, by choosing the Settings options in the app. Some of the settings you will be able to manage include the connection and updating of your Wi-Fi network on the Amazon Echo, and you can also adjust the Bluetooth pairing options.

If you have a remote control, you will find the option to pair or unpaired the remote with the Amazon Echo. The Alexa app also facilitates some personalization features so that you are better able to relate to what the app has to offer. You can begin personalizing your Echo by changing the name of your device. In addition, you can also adjust your wake word, as well as the sounds that the Amazon Echo will use as you give it your chosen commands.

Furthermore, you are able to input your address for the location of your device, as this will make it easier to provide you with location based information, such as the correct time, the weather forecast, and the places of interest that may be close to where you are. This is also important for the news.

Other settings include metric measurements, which will allow you to choose between Metric and U.S. conversions based on what makes you more comfortable, and the Voicecast, which is able to send information that you have heard from your Amazon Echo to your Fire tablet, as long as it has been linked with your account on Amazon.

Using The Wake Word

For the voice command, you have to use a wake word in order to set the device ready to execute your orders. Amazon Echo comes with Alexa as its wake word, which can be changed by the user to a name they would prefer.

This wake word can be used in any room in a house, not necessarily in the room where the device is. Your Echo will always be listening out so the moment you use the wake word, it will be ready to take your command. It is also able to receive commands from any direction. You will see it illuminate once you use the wake word, and this means that it is already alert.

Alexa is able to receive sounds and commands very clearly and does not miss out on any command, even if you speak in a hurry or many people speak at the same time. It is also very clear when giving a response.

There might be an instance where you do want the device to be silent completely, and not to respond to anything even though you may say the wake word by mistake. In this instance, you can use the mute button that is located on the top of your echo. When you press this button, the light ring will turn red in color, causing Alexa to go mute. To make your Amazon Echo interactive once more, all you need is to press the button again.

This capability comes in handy when you may be having a serious discussion or important meeting, and do not want to be interrupted by your always listening Echo, which may provide you with facts or information as you hold your discussion.

After getting the Amazon Echo now is the time to use it. Obviously, you don't want to just be using the device for commands that are just too simple. However, before you get to the complex stuff, let's first understand some simple yet handy tricks for using the device that will transform you from a beginner to a pro user in the shortest time possible.

How to Change your Wake Word

Engage the Alexa app on the mobile device.

Select "Settings" from the left-hand navigation menu.

Within the Settings menu select the Echo device whose "wake" word you wish to change.

Once you have selected the device, scroll down the settings menu until you see "Wake Word." Select it.

Choose a different "Wake Word" from the drop down menu.

Voice Training Your Echo: How to Make Alexa Smarter

The key to getting your Amazon Echo to work effectively is to ensure that you give Alexa commands that she can understand and carry out. Alexa has been primed to learn her new owner, understand preferences, and recognize a voice. In addition, the features that she has are meant to make one's life considerably easier and more convenient. In a way, they are to lead to what can be termed as a seamless experience. However, this does not occur automatically as there are trainings that need to be done.

Every Amazon Echo features the Voice Training Option, which can be found on the main menu of the Alexa App. You should install this app onto your primary mobile device for ease of accessibility to certain functions on your Echo.

Once you are in the Voice Training Option, you will find that there are 25 phrases that have been pre-determined for speaking to Alexa. All these phrases are different, and you will go through a session where you say them to Alexa repeatedly, usually for approximately 15 minutes. The reason for this is so that the device is able to fully understand your pronunciation of words, and the patterns of your speech. It will also be able to discern what you are saying based on your accent.

Every command that you give to the Amazon Echo needs to begin with the word Alexa. The following options express how you should command Alexa:

Alexa, play some dancehall music.

Alexa, stop the alarm.

Alexa, snooze for five minutes.

Alexa, what is the weather today?

Alexa, tell me the latest news headlines.

Alexa, increase the volume.

Alexa, tell me the time.

Alexa, pair Bluetooth.

Alexa, add sugar to my shopping list.

Alexa, start a to-do list.

Alexa, who is winning the Cubs game?

Alexa, who is Donald Trump?

Alexa, how fattening is a large bowl of spaghetti Bolognese?

There are so many different things that you can ask Alexa about, and she has answers to all of them. She can even play certain games for you, and carry out certain actions. For example, when making a bet with someone, you can ask Alexa to toss a coin and she will help you easily choose between heads and tails. She is an excellent assistant, who, the more you interact with, the more you are likely to depend on for all your information.

You may find that there are instances when Alexa does not fully understand what you are trying to communicate. When this happens, it is possible to go over your voice interaction with Alexa through the Alexa App. You would need to go to History, and then to settings. Here, you will find that your interactions have been arranged based on the request that you have given, or in order of questions.

When you choose one of the entries, you will be able to listen to it again. This will help you to determine if there were errors in anything that you said. Furthermore, it will also be possible to evaluate a translation of what Alexa understood, which will simplify for you what the issue may be.

Note: In an earlier section, we saw that Alexa's ability to adapt to different speech patterns and accents is one of the key things that place her above competitors such as Microsoft's Cortana and Apple's Siri.

As an artificial intelligence, Alexa learns from her environment. For her to understand your voice clearly and easily regardless of your accent or speech pattern, you have to voice train her. By ensuring that Alexa recognizes and understands your normal speaking voice (remember Amazon advocates for speaking to Alexa in a normal manner), you can greatly improve your user experience with the device and make Alexa smarter in the process.

Why You Should Voice Train Alexa

The voice assistant field or business is still in its infancy. Therefore, Alexa, like all voice assistants available today is not perfect. There are times when your commands will be incomprehensible to her or yield unintended results.

However, with training, which coincidentally takes a few minutes, Alexa can easily understand your pronunciations and learn to recognize your voice regardless of any noise interference in the room.

Fortunately, voice training your Alexa is easy. Before we look at how to do it, let's start by looking at how to prepare for the voice training session.

Preparing For Voice Training

Before you commence voice training Alexa, you want to simulate the exact atmosphere where you'll place your Echo. You want to train her under normal conditions. For instance, if your Echo is placed somewhere in your sitting area and you primarily intend to issue commands from across the room or in the kitchen that is what you want to simulate during training.

Further, you don't need to go out of your way to accommodate Alexa by speaking in a more precise and clear manner. You want to speak to her in your normal voice. You also don't want to be too close to the speaker microphones, or use the microphone in-built into the remote. You want the voice training to simulate a normal day setting. In a normal setting, your voice will not be close to the microphones and your speech pattern will be different at different times. For example, when you're tired, your voice will be lower. On the other hand, when you're excited, your voice will be higher.

While you want to simulate a normal day during training, you should also make a point of limiting background noise interference. For example, you don't want to voice train Alexa with the TV or radio on. You want to ensure Alexa can hear your voice clearly.

How to Start Training Your Echo

Once your environmental settings are right and you are ready to get rolling with the training, fire up your Alexa app on the primary control device. Once the app is up and running, select the hamburger menu in the upper left corner as shown in the diagram below, and navigate to voice training.

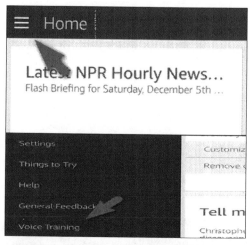

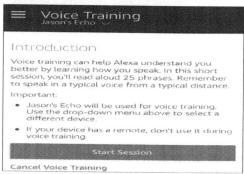

If you have more than one echo connected to your Amazon Account, the image may not be immediately visible. Instead, the app may ask you to select the Echo you want to train. However, you should note that if you have more than one Echo device, training the Echo closest to you would make it easier for Alexa to understand you as long as the devices are connected to the same Amazon Prime Account. After selecting the Echo you want to voice train, select the start session option to get started with the voice training.

When you commence the session, the ring at the top of your Echo will light up, and prompts will appear on the app and ask you to read them in a slide-show manner. Read each phrase as normally as you can and press next if you're satisfied with the result. If the results are not very satisfactory, you can opt to repeat the phrase as shown in the figure below.

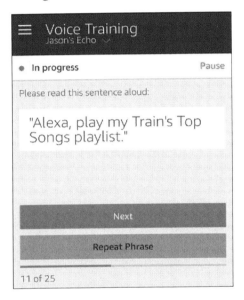

Note: When most of us read something on a screen, we often do it in a voice different from the one we use in normal everyday conversations. Therefore, instead of reading the phrases off the app, read each phrase, memorize it, look away from the screen or close your eyes, and utter the phrase in a natural tone of voice or as if you were talking to someone within earshot. Go through each phrase until you are done with the voice training.

In total, there're 25 phrases. If at the end of the training session you're not satisfied with Alexa's comprehension of your voice and pronunciations, you can always repeat the process at any given time to fine tune your results. However, since Alexa is ever connected to the internet and the Amazon cloud, it is highly unlikely you'll need multiple training sessions.

How to conduct a Voice Training Session

✓ Open the Alexa Application.

✓ Click the left navigation panel and select "Settings."

✓ Select "Voice Training."

✓ Tap "Start Session."

✓ Speak the phrase of your choice into the app then select "Next."

(Need to repeat a phrase? Select "Pause" and then "Repeat Phrase")

✓ You have reached the end of your session. Select "Complete."

(If you need to end your session anytime hit "Pause" then "End Session.")

Set Up the Alexa Skills Event Source

✓ You need to log into the AWS Console then migrate to AWS Lambda
✓ Tap the list to access the configuration elements.
✓ You need to choose the events tab
✓ Tap the add event source
✓ Choose Alexa skills set from the event source type
✓ Now you have to tap "submit."

How to make an AWS Lambda Function for a custom skill

✓   You can take out some of the complexity of managing and setting up your endpoint by using a Lambda function for your service.

✓   You don't have to manage/administer any computer resources for the service and you don't need to verify services that are coming from Lambda. This is done for you by permissions within AWS.

✓   You don't have to run servers all the time because AWS Lambda runs your code and scales it up with higher use.

✓   Alexa will encrypt your communications with Lambda by using TLS.

✓   The Lambda free tier is ample enough for your function assisting an Alexa skill. The free tier will let you use the first million requests each month. The free tier function will not expire, but you can use it indefinitely.

✓   AWS assists your code written in Node.js (Java Script), Java and Python. Go ahead and copy and edit Java and Python within the inline code editor in the AWS Lambda console. Or you can upload it in a zip file.

✓   If you want to do basic testing, then engage your function manually by sending it JSON requests in the Lambda console.

✓   Lambda functions must coordinate with the same service interface and handle the same three types of requests Alexa does.

✓   Your Lambda functions for your Alexa skills must be hosted out of the U.S East (N. Virginia Region).They are the only Lambda region the Alexa Skills kit supports, so you need to contact them for any Lambda kit support requests.

✓   Note: The instructions following cover creating a new Lambda function for a custom skill.

How you can make a Lambda Function for an Alexa Skill

✓   If you haven't already, go to Amazon Web Services and make an account.

✓   Tap into the AWS management console and migrate to AWS Lambda.

✓   Tap on the region drop down menu in the upper right corner and click the N Virginia Region.

✓   If you don't have Lambda functions yet, click" Get Started Now." If you do, then click "Create a Lambda function."

✓   Start with a simple code in Node Java Script or Python. You either choose Alexa-skills—kit-color-expert or Alexa –skills-kit-Color-Python blueprint. Type "Alexa" in the filter box then you will be able to filter the type of blueprints.

✓   Select the "Alexa Skill set" for the event source type. Hit "Next."

✓   Put in a name and description for your function.

✓   Select the language you want to use for the runtime (Node JavaScript, Python or Java).

✓   If you choose Java to be sure you load your Java code in a zip file.

✓   Be careful – once you "save" a language for a function it cannot be changed.

✓   You need to set the task to a basic execution role. This sets the parameters that the AWS resource function can access. The review page should have Alexa as the event source.

✓   Click "Create Function" to save your new function.

✓   If you want to add your code, edit the function and select the "Code" tab. By doing this, you will be able to do the following:

•Write your code right into the editor in Lambda console (use Node Java Script or Python).

•Write code offline and copy and paste it right into your Lambda console center (use Node JavaScript or Python).

•Write your code offline and load it to the Lambda function in a zip file (use Node Java Script, Python or Java).

•Use the Eclipse IDE and the AWS Toolkit for Eclipse (use Java).

Now Test Your Lambda Function in the Console

Go to the function list and click the function name to open the details for it.

✓ Now click the Test button. If this is your first time clicking this test button, the input sample dialog box will be displayed.

✓ Tap on the sample event template list and choose one of the three following sample Alexa request:

• The Alexa Start Session
• The Alexa Intent – My Colors
• The Alexa End Session

✓ You can migrate one of these requests as-is or use it at ground zero to try various intent and slot values.

✓ Finally, tap "Submit".

✓ Now that the function has run, the Execution section will show the response returned by your function selection. It will show it in JSON format. The response should coordinate with the request you pasted in the "Sample Event Box."

Below is a sample of a "Launch Request" the sample would return on a request like this:

```
{
  "version": "1.0",
  "sessionAttributes": {},
  "response": {
    "outputSpeech": {
      "type": "PlainText",
```

```
    "text": "Welcome to the Alexa Skills Kit sample, Please tell me
your favorite color by saying, my favorite color is red."
    },
    "card": {
     "type": "Simple",
     "title": "Session Speechlet - Welcome",
     "content": "Session Speechlet - Welcome to the Alexa Skills Kit
sample, Please tell me your favorite color by saying, my favorite color
is red"
    },
    "reprompt": {
     "output Speech": {
      "type": "Plain Text",
      "text": "Please tell me your favorite color by saying, my favorite
color is red"
     }
    },
    "should End Session": false
   }
}
```

✓The execution log section show any log messages generated by the
code. The sample will write a log message for each sort of request. It
should look something like this:

2015-05-18T23:53:22.357Z   0f885f98-fdb9-11e4-80af-
1b9f8363b496   on Intent requestId=amzn1.echo-
api.request.6919844a-733e-4e89-893a-fdcb77e2ef0d,
sessionId=amzn1.echo-api.session.abeee1a7-aee0-41e6-8192-
e6faaed9f5ef

You can add the Alexa Skills Kit Event Source

Adding this Alexa skills kit event source allows Alexa the necessary
invocation permissions for the function.
By creating the Lambda function using either Alexa-skills-kit-color-
expert or Alexa-skills-kit-color-expert-python blueprint your function
is established. You can skip the steps below:

✓   First, you will need to Log in to AWS console and migrate to AWS Lambda.

✓   Tap your function in your list to open the configuration data.

✓   Choose the "Event Sources" tab.

✓   Tap "Add event source."

✓   Choose "Alexa Skills Kit" from the "Event Source Type."

✓   Hit the "Submit" button.

Note. You should limit invocation permissions to Alexa. If you follow this recommendation, you will limit the number of malicious callers to this function.

Sample Connection Model for your Color Expert Blueprint Model
If you chose to create your Lambda function using either the Alexa-skills-kit-color-expert or Alexa-skills-kit-color-expert-python blueprint, then go ahead and test your device with an Alexa-enabled device or a Service Simulator. Here is how to do this: Register your skill in the developer portal and then give an interaction model for the new skill.

☐ Here is the Intent Schema:

```
{
  "intents": [
    {
      "intent": "MyColorIsIntent",
      "slots": [
        {
          "name": "Color",
          "type": "LIST_OF_COLORS"
        }
      ]
    },
    {
      "intent": "WhatsMyColorIntent"
    },
    {
      "intent": "AMAZON.HelpIntent"
```

```
      }
   ]
}
```

Have a look at the Custom Slot type:
First, you will want to create LIST OF COLORS and paste in the following values:
green
red
blue
orange
gold
silver
yellow
black
white

Here are some sample expressions:
WhatsMyColorIntent what's my favorite color
WhatsMyColorIntent what is my favorite color
WhatsMyColorIntent what's my color
WhatsMyColorIntent what is my color
WhatsMyColorIntent my color
WhatsMyColorIntent my favorite color
WhatsMyColorIntent get my color
WhatsMyColorIntent get my favorite color
WhatsMyColorIntent gives me my favorite color
WhatsMyColorIntent gives me my color
WhatsMyColorIntent what my color is
WhatsMyColorIntent what my favorite color is
WhatsMyColorIntent yes
WhatsMyColorIntent yup
WhatsMyColorIntent sure
WhatsMyColorIntent yes, please
MyColorIsIntent my favorite color is {Color}

How to Build Custom Skills

✓ You need to design a voice user interface.

✓ This is the critical step in building your skill. Do this before you build any code. Users will primarily interface with this when they interact with your skill.

✓ Make a flow diagram that illustrates how users will interface with the skill. Your flow diagram should show any potential requests users may make. Also, include possible outcomes of these requests. This diagram will be used when you create the detailed elements of your interface.

✓ Create your intent schema, which is a JSON structure, that declares intents your service can accept and handle. Use the flow diagram tour service.

✓ Design a set of expressions that will map your requests. These are the expressions your users could say when they are relating to your skill.

Set up the Skill

✓ The below steps outline how to create a skill in the developer portal, and you will learn to create your service to seat your code.

✓ You need to register your skill on the developer portal and you need to create a name and invocation name for your new skill.

✓ You should manufacture an AWS Lambda function (a web service offering from Amazon) for the quickest start. You can run code in the cloud without managing servers with the Lambda function.

✓ You can also build your skill with any web service and host it with any cloud provider.

Write and Test your Skill code.

✓Primarily, with your coding task for your skill, you want to create a service that can accept requests from Alexa. You should be able to send back responses.

✓ Now write your code for your skill. If you are using Lambda, you can code in Node Java Script, Java or Python. If you decide to host your skill as a web service than you can use any programming language.

✓ Go to the developer portal and fill in the rest of the information for the skill for testing. This means you have to add the endpoint (Lambda ARN if using Lambda), the intent schema, and your expressions.

✓Test your skill with a Service Simulator or Alexa device.

Submit Your Skill

✓Finish your skill and submit it for certification so it will be available for Amazon customers.

✓Update your data for your skill displayed in the Alexa App.

✓ Test this skill against the submission checklist. The checklist includes tests performed by the certification team. You can speed up your certification process if you can pass all their tests.

✓ Complete the testing and submit your skill for certification.

The Skills that you find on the Amazon Echo refer to the capabilities that have been voice-driven. The Alexa Skills Kit is integral to adding revolutionary skills to the Amazon Echo, making it more useful for the customer. It is possible to create and develop your own 'skill' using the Alexa Skills Kit, which will allow you to use customized voice commands for what you choose.

To begin with, you will need to define intents. The intents are a part of what is known as your voice interface, which is what will map out what your user says with the intent that you want Echo to handle, through the cloud.

This requires you to provide two inputs. The first one will provide information on which intents that the service you are creating can be accepted and processed. It takes up a JSON structure and is referred to as the Intent Schema. The second one deals with the Spoken Input Data and is split into two capabilities.

The first one provides a text file that is structured and which includes a sample of utterances. These will help to connect the intents to the phrases, which may be spoken. The second one provides custom values, which will represent particular items that your skills shall be utilized.

As they develop, you can then input this information into a developed portal, which can be found on the Interaction Model page on the Amazon Echo website.

When working with your Alexa Skills Kit, remember to keep in mind the final user and the way that they will essentially use the skill. Their use shall usually be question based using certain phrases to make a request. The phrases that are commonly used include ask....to, ask....when, ask....for, and tell....to. By using the right phrases, you will find that it is easy to define the voice interface for the skill that you are creating using the kit. Remember that the length of the conversation through the exchange of phrases will also determine any other words that you need to consider as the customer's response.

There should be prompts available for words or commands, which are not recognized to ensure that your skill is interactive and easy to use. These may include repeating a prompt or even ending a conversation.

For you to adequately create these new skills using the Alexa Skills Kit, there are several things that you need to have in place. The first is to be registered on the developer portal through an account. Next, you should be able to create as well as deploy a cloud-based service. Finally, there is a need for a development environment, which takes into consideration the language that you will be using. Java, Node.js and most web service languages are used for creating skills.

Once you have completed creating your skill, you should take the time to test it thoroughly using your device. The moment that you ensure it meets your requirements, you can then deploy the skill into a cloud using the AWS Lambda, which is offered by Amazon, or choose to host the skill yourself using a web service.

With the passage of time, the Alexa Skills Kit continues to improve and include features, which are based on what the customers have requested. Some of the features that have been incorporated as built-in intents include stop, cancel, and help. These are essential for developers in delivering what consumers need, and should be included in the skills. The reason being that they will allow for Alexa to give a response when a customer asks for an action to be brought to a halt. Furthermore, should there be a need for assistance; it is also possible when the skill is running.

How to Configure a New Home Smart Skill

Open the Amazon Developer Portal in your browser and log in.

Migrate to the Alexa section by clicking "Apps and Services." Now click Alexa in the top navigation.

Find the Alexa skill tests box and click "Get Started."

Click the "Add New Skill Button."

On the Skill Data page, select "Smart Home Skill API," and enter the name for your skill.

Click "Save" and now copy the skill application ID to the clipboard.

You can finish registering your Skill Set in the Developer Portal

First, you must configure OAuth 2.0 for your skill. Do this by logging in with Amazon or another provider if you wish.

Go back to your skill in the Developer Portal. To accomplish this, login and navigate to the Alexa section by clicking Apps and Services. Next, click Alexa in the top navigation. Select your skill on the displayed list.

Click past the Interaction tab. The communication model, which is what you can say to engage the Smart Home Skill API, is predetermined, so it doesn't need to be identified. For features of the smart home voice interaction model, see the expressions shown with each reference entry in the Smart Home Skill API Reference.

Locate the Configuration page, in the Endpoint field, and copy in the ARN number from the Lambda function you made.

You also must engage Account Linking for your skill. This allows users to link their cloud-enabled devices with the Alexa skill, which is why you will need OAuth 2.0 information for the device cloud your skill talks with. To find more information about linking your account, see Linking an Alexa User with a User in Your System. It's very important to note that the OAuth provider must have a certificate signed by an Amazon-approved certificate authority, or linking of the account will fail.

You need these fields:

✓Authorization URL: This will be your URL for your web site's login page. Refer to Enabling Account Linking Support to Your Login Page for Data about how this page is used when clients connect the accounts.

✓Client ID: A benchmark the login page utilizes to see that the request came from your skill. This value is transferred to your authorization URL in the client_id area. You will use authorization code grant, which translates this value, and is also part of the client credentials that the Alexa service includes when asking for an access token from the Access Token URI.

✓Reroute URL: When your account is connecting it displays the Redirect URL, which is the URL to which your login page must redirect the user after they are authorized. The URL should be whitelisted with the OAuth provider.

✓Authorization Grant Type: Authorization Code Grant is predetermined, and it's the supported grant type for Smart Home Skill API.

For Authorization Code Grant, you should fill in the following:

Access Token URI: This is the URL for the OAuth server that supplies the access tokens.

Client Secret: A credential you give that lets the Alexa service authorize in conjunction with the Access Token URI. This will be combined with the Client ID to say the request is coming from Alexa.

Client Authorized Scheme: Locates the type of authentication Alexa should use when asking for tokens from the Access Token URI.

Privacy Policy URL: A URL for a page with the privacy policy. This connection is shown in the Alexa app and is required for smart home skills.

On the Test page, make sure that your skill is enabled for testing by choosing "Yes."

Now let's test your skill:

When your implementation is finished, and you've tried the skill adapter in Lambda, you can try the smart home skill. The user will test his skill with an Alexa-enabled device. Follow these steps:

Make sure the event source is on for your skill adapter.

In the Lambda console, choose the smart home skill, and on the Event Sources tab, choose the Alexa Smart Home event source.

If the State is enabled, no action is required. If the state is Disabled, click Disabled and then click Enable.

Locate your skill in the Alexa app, enable it and account-link your skill to the device cloud it is supposed to work with. Find your skill in the Alexa app. Find "Skills" and enter your smart home skill in the search box. To remove your account-linking later disable your skill in the "Skills" tab.

Discover and manage your devices in the "Devices" section in the "Smart home" tab of the Alexa app.

You can give Alexa commands using the utterances that your skills will support with device names you have set for your devices that you have linked in your account-linked device cloud. Make sure you test the skill with valid utterances and wrong ones, and in a variety of conditions such as "target device powered off."

If you are satisfied with your smart home skill's performance, submit it for certification.

Submit your skill for certification

Now your final step is to get your skill certified. This way it will appear on the skills tab of the Alexa app and everyone can use your skill. To get it certified follow these steps:

Descriptions: Finish the Short Skill and Full Skill descriptions.

Category: This is automatically set to Smart Home and can't be changed.

Keywords: (optional) Add keywords appropriate for your skill.

Images: Add small and large icons per the guidelines specified.

Add any testing instructions necessary for the certification team.

Click Next.

Go to the Privacy and Compliance page and answer the questions, then click "Submit for Certification."

Alexa Fund Investments

In addition to the ways that these productive tasks that Amazon Echo is able to carry out, through the investments that the Alexa fund has carried out, there are more fun capabilities for the Amazon Echo in the near future. The companies that receive the funding are not chosen at random. The selections are based on companies that have proven they put the customer before all else, especially when it comes to voice operated products.

In addition, the companies need to have creative products, which are being used to resolve issues that customers are facing to make life smoother. They need to have a vision for expansion, so that they can build on any innovation that they incorporate with Alexa. Finally, the applications need to be unique, especially when it relates to voice technology. From these criteria, there is a range of companies that have successfully made the cut. These include the following:

Rachio

In line with building up the ultimate smart home, the Alexa Fund is offering support to Rachio, a software and hardware company that creates products for better water efficiency within the home. Using the Alexa Skills Kit, it should be possible to create a new skill that Alexa can use to automatically control an intelligent sprinkler. With Alexa, Rachio will be able to water certain areas of the garden, or a timer can be set for watering at specific times. The commands that can be used include, 'Alexa, tell Rachio that the grass needs more water today,'

Petnet

This company has created the SmartFeeder. For people with pets who are interested in the overall health and eating patterns of their pets, this device includes an app which is easily able to keep track of the meals that the pet consumes, including the amounts eaten and how often they are eaten. With its integration, the Amazon Echo will be able to let pet owners know what the right portion for their pets shall be, as well as what ingredients are recommended for the pet based on its weight and age, and how active it is. It will respond to commands like, 'Alexa, how much has Rover eaten today?'

Musaic

Amazon Echo is at heart a brilliant speaker, though it is limited to playing music in only one room. Musaic is a HiFi system with high-resolution and is also wireless. This system, however, enables a listener to experience music in each room within the home, and it also has the ability to connect with smart lighting. By using the Alexa Voice Service, it shall create a skill where customers are able to control the Musaic system that they currently have with voice.

Garageio

This takes your smart home out to the garage, with a system in place to control and to know the continued status of the door for your garage. The company has a product that is called the Blackbox. This product is able to manage the operations of a garage door opened. The Alexa Skills Kit is being used with this product to help alert a customer whether the door of the garage has been opened. Furthermore, Alexa is able to send messages to Garageio to control the door. A command that could be used includes, 'Alexa, ask Garageio, is the garage door closed?'

Toymail

Being able to communicate with your child has always been important, and the company Toymail has a range of toys, which enable parents and their children to easily communicate with each other, without having to use a smartphone. The parents are able to speak to their children through a toy, which connects with the internet, and houses a microphone and speaker. The toy is called the Mailman. The Alexa Skills Kit allows a parent to send a message to their child through a skill that has been developed. The message will be sent using Toymail. This company shall also use the Alexa Voice Service in its development. A command that can be used includes, 'Alexa, send a Toymail to Richard...I will be home at 3 pm this afternoon so that we can bake cookies together.'

Invoxia

Invoxia is a company that creates Wi-Fi communication devices, which are found within the kitchen. The device is referred to as Triby, and it is able to magnetically stick onto a fridge. These devices are able to execute a myriad of interactive tasks including playing music, displaying messages and listening to phone calls. By integrating with the Alexa Voice Service and the Alexa Skills Kit, it becomes possible for customers to remotely command these services to be used. A customer may give a command like, 'Alexa, ask Triby to call the office.'

Orange Chef

The Amazon Echo works excellently as a kitchen timer, and its services can be extended to do even more within the kitchen. That is due to its investment in Orange Chef, a company that has created a product that is referred to as Countertop. This product is able to connect to electronics in the kitchen, such as slow cookers and blenders, and then keeps track of the ingredients within these devices. To improve the services, the Alexa Voice Services shall be incorporated so that customers are able to ask Alexa questions like, 'Alexa, how many calories are in this juice,' and the customer can get a response. This will make cooking so much easier, as the hands remain free to focus on the dishes, rather than on lots of other aspects.

Campbell's Soup

Since the Amazon Echo is so useful in the kitchen, Campbell's soup has increased how useful the Echo can be. This is because the company wanted to find a way to get more people to cook using their available products. So, if you ask Alexa for recipes, she is able recommend some that use Campbell's products, making these the first company to represent a food brand on the Echo. This is possible through the Campbell Kitchen app.

Furthermore, the available recipes are based on the profile of the user and other information that has been collated by the Echo during its use. In addition, the recipes are also based on the seasons as well as the trends taking place in food. When a customer asks Alexa for a recipe, it is also sent to the email of the person who gave the request.

Dragon Innovation

This is an excellent collaboration between Dragon Innovation and the Alexa Skills Kit as well as the Alexa Voice Service. The reason, being that Dragon Innovation offers a range of services, as well as products, which are used by hardware start-ups. It allows developers to incorporate Alexa's capabilities in any stage of production, starting from the prototype and going all the way to sales.

Scout Alarm

This company offers customizable systems for home security through what they call the Scout System. It includes a range of services, which include motion detectors and entry sensors. The Alexa Skills Kit has been used to get the Echo to integrate with this system, allowing a person to arm the alarm when they need to without needing to press any buttons. You can give a command like, 'Alexa, arm Sleep Mode.'

Insteon Hub

The Amazon Echo started off with Philips Hub to incorporate it with lighting systems, and now there is another company that has formed a collaboration, and that is Insteon. So, with your Insteon hub controlled lighting, you can use the commands through Alexa for remote control. You can give voice commands to switch off the lights, as well as to dim them.

Mojio

In addition to helping develop an ideal smart home, the Amazon Echo also has a role to play in ensuring that your car can provide you with detailed information. The Alexa Skills Kit is being used by Mojio, which is a company that develops connected car solutions. It will become possible to ask Alexa to extract information on the driving performance as well as the status of on-board systems and more. Alexa will be able to provide information to commands such as, 'Alexa, where is my son driving the car this morning,' or 'Alexa, do I need to put in more gas today?' This helps you to plan and be more efficient, even before you have left your home.

Mara

Alexa will also be able to help you with your fitness and training due to the integration of the Alexa Skills Kit and the Alexa Voice Service with Mara. Mara gives information on your fitness performance and training as you go through your exercises, and is able to play the role of your personal trainer. With the Echo, you will be able to source information on your progress by asking questions like, 'Alexa, how many miles have I ran today?'

All the companies that are receiving the funds, so far, are useful both inside and outside of the home, and add considerably to what Alexa is able to deliver. The skills are part of what makes using Alexa so exciting.

Finding all these skills can be a challenge, especially if you know what skill that you want, but may not know what the company is called. Using the app, it becomes possible to find just what you need. To find these skills, and even more which are up and coming, use your smart phone and select the Alexa app. From the menu that appears, choose the option skills. You will see a list of all the skills available; all you need to do is scroll through and find the one that you want and choose Enable. You will be directed to practice some example phrases, following which, you will be able to use the skill with Alexa without any problems.

Although, the Amazon Echo has been on the market for a relatively short period, it has been becoming more productive with the passage of time. The skills discussed in this section touch on what is currently available and this gives an indication of the direction of growth that the Echo is heading to. It is likely that in the future, the Echo shall become even more useful, making it easily applicable in your daily life as an assistant that you cannot live without.

Now that you have a good understanding of how to use the Amazon Echo, it is now time to move on to the more specific stuff that will help you unleash the Amazon Echo super-user in you.

Simple Tricks You Can Try with Your Amazon Echo

Change its wake word if you do not like using Alexa. You can do this as many times as you want.

If you do not want your device to do anything for you even by accident, use the mute button to silence it. This can be done if you do not wish to record anything at a given time. The button is at the top of the device and once you press it long enough, a red light will illuminate, meaning, it will not say or respond to anything until you press the same key once more to activate its back.

Access your device from the web easily through the Echo Amazon website. If you are unable to access it through your android or iOS device, the web will do.

You can link the prime accounts of your family members to the device too, through the Amazon Echo website Household feature. The family members need to have these prime accounts to start with. Then, they can download the Echo app to their smart devices for them to access and join the Household.

Use your device for simple math calculations. You do not have to go through the hassle of calculations if you are close to your device. Your Amazon Echo will easily execute quick addition and subtraction, as well as being able to calculate numbers that contain decimals. Just ask through a voice command and she will give you the answer.

You can have the device repeat a response for as long as you want. If you have not heard the answer the first time, just command it to repeat the answer and you will have it.

If you have any problem with your Amazon Echo, help is always closer than you think. Seek help faster through the Amazon Echo website and someone will respond to your problem immediately. Just type in your number and someone will call you ready to help.

Take the time to load all your favorite music onto the Amazon Cloud Player, which will make it easier for you to hear exactly what you want when you ask Alexa. You can include up to 250 songs for an amazing playlist. This in addition to your Amazon Prime music library access will bring out the best from this appliance.

This chapter reveals something integral about the Amazon Echo i.e. it is highly convenient and easy to use. By being able to access this device hands-free, it conveniently fits into your busy daily life, allowing you to do more tasks in a shorter period.

Tips And Tricks For Using Amazon Echo At The Highest Potential

Once you have your Amazon Echo, you should ensure that you make good use of it so that you can benefit from all that it has to offer. Amazon Echo is one of those devices that will do quite a bit for you so realizing its full potential will make you a happier Echo user for a very long time.

The key to getting the most out of your Amazon Echo is to understand exactly what it can do for you, and for that, you need to start making friends with Alexa. Alexa is what your Echo is all about. She is the assistant that speaks to you and the one you will interact with. Alexa seems real; she is easy to understand and sometimes, depending on what you ask, she will reveal an astonishing sense of humor.

Alexa is able to offer you entertainment as she answers questions you ask in unexpected ways. This means that she offers ideal interaction with all members of the family. She is able to offer teaching as she directly links with online encyclopedias such as Wikipedia.

With seven microphones fitted within the device, Alexa is able to clearly hear you, usually from any part of the room that you may speak to her from. Once she is used to your voice, she will be able to easily pick it up and carry out your commands, even when there is some background noise in the room. The best thing about Alexa is her ability to listen to and respond to any commands that you give her. This capability is most useful in the Amazon Echo. With so many commands to try with Alexa, you will definitely need some time and persistence to get to unleash the device's full power.

Shop on Amazon

If you are an Amazon Prime member, shopping on Amazon becomes exceptionally simple with the voice activated Amazon Echo. All that you need to do is tell Alexa to reorder the products of your choosing from Amazon, and she will be able to do this for you with ease. This saves you significant time on your PC, and enables you to get your products at your convenience just the way that you are used to. So how can you do this? Here is how:

How to Set Up Automatic Purchases on Your Amazon Echo

Alexa is profoundly useful. One of its uses is the ability to automate Amazon shopping. With Alexa, you can complete purchase orders by voice commands using the default payment method on your Amazon account.

With voice purchasing, you can manage your shopping setting and chose to have voice purchasing on or off, or require a confirmation code before the completion of a purchase.

How to Setup Voice Purchasing

With Alexa, you can place orders from the digital music store. Further, if you're an Amazon prime account holder. To set up voice purchasing, fire up the Alexa app on your phone, scroll through the left navigation panel, and find the settings tab. Here, select voice purchasing and select an option to update or change.

Enable Voice Purchasing

✓ Open your Alexa app on your smartphone or echoamazon.com while you're logged on to the account that controls the Echo.

✓ Migrate to "Settings" in the left-hand menu and select "Voice Purchasing."

✓   There is a switch by "Voice Purchasing" Toggle it "on" to enable voice purchasing.

Disabling Voice Purchasing

✓Simply toggle off the switch by voice purchasing and it's deactivated.

To activate or deactivate voice purchasing, use the switch to toggle voice purchasing on or off. To set up 'require confirmation code' enter your preferred 4-digit code and save the changes. When you set up this option, Alexa will prompt for the 4-digit code before completing a voice purchase. If you're worried about your pass code privacy, don't be; Alexa does not store the code in your voice history. When creating your confirmation code, Amazon advices against using a code usable across multiple platforms or services, i.e. create a unique code rather than using one you use on multiple services or accounts.

When Alexa carries out voice command purchases, she does so through your default 1-click payment system available on Amazon. You can change these settings by simply heading over to the amazon homepage, setting, and updating your 1-click payment option as well as billing.

Voice Purchasing Requirements

Once you've ironed out that, to automate voice shopping, for different items, you need: For all digital music orders from the music store, you need a verified payment method, and a U.S billing address. For physical products purchases from Amazon, you need to sign up for the Amazon Prime membership free trial or have an annual prime subscription, as well as a U.S billing address and a verified payment system.

Going About Digital Music Purchases on Alexa

When you make digital music orders via Alexa's voice command, the purchases are stored on your Amazon music library free of charge (there is no limit on the amount of digital storage space available for prime music purchases). The icing on the cake is that all these purchases are compatible with all devices registered to work with your Amazon account, and are available for download and playback on all compatible devices. If you're a prime account holder, you can add prime music to your library at no extra cost.

Going About Physical Product Purchases on Alexa

Amazon prime account holders can ask Alexa to re-order items from their order history. The caveat to this is that you can only do this for prime-eligible items. If you're worried about multiple purchases, don't be. When Alexa finds the item you want, she gives you the option to cancel or confirm the order. Further, if similar items are available for prime-order, and you decline purchase of the first item, Alexa will offer the second item as an alternative and ask for confirmation.

When Alexa searches your order history, cannot find the requested item, or fails to complete purchase for whatever reason, Amazon's choice might make a suggestion. This suggestion will be of well-priced, highly rated items available for prime shipping.

How to reorder Prime-Eligible Items with Alexa

As indicated earlier, to order physical items with Alexa, a 30-day free trial Amazon Prime Membership, or annual prime membership, a verified payment method, and a U.S billing address are mandatory. Further, Alexa process the orders using the 1-click payment available on your Amazon account (physical product offers are eligible for free returns).

To command Alexa into placing an order, say, "Reorder [item name]. This will prompt Alexa to search all previous orders for the item and provide a response. If she finds the item, she offers you the option to confirm or cancel the order and provides relevant details of the item [details such as price and shipping] in the Alexa app.

If she finds more than one similar item, she will offer you the second item as an alternative if you decline to confirm purchase of the first item. If she finds multiple similar items, Alex will display details of these items on the Alexa app.

Enjoy Amazon Prime Music

With Amazon Echo, you have full access to Amazon prime music. You only need to subscribe to it, and you can always enjoy your favorite hits through your voice-command device. To enjoy this music, just ask Alexa to play you a particular song, a song from a certain musician or a specific genre of music that you prefer and it shall be done. The prime music library is full of great music that subscribers from across the world enjoy; and so, you will always get something that you will enjoy listening to. With just one command, you will be enjoying great music through an incredible speaker and with high quality.

Your family members are also able to enjoy the same music through their Prime accounts. So how do you buy digital music on Amazon?

How to Buy Digital Music with Alexa

Buying music with Alexa is a breeze and a lot of fun. As indicated earlier, all your digital purchases use the 1-click payment method on your Amazon account.

To buy music and keep it, you can opt to shop for singular songs, or by album, or by artist. To shop for a song, say "shop for the song... [Song name]

To shop for an album say, "shop for the album [album title]"

To shop for song by artist, say, "shop for songs by [artist name] or "shop for new songs by [artist name]

Once you find the song you want, add it to the currently playing sample by saying, "Add this [song/album] to my library. To buy the song, simply say "buy this [song/album]. If you are a prime member and the item is available for prime music purchase at no additional cost, Alexa will notify you before confirming purchase.

What to Do When You Place an Accidental Order

As you navigate your Echo and integrate it into your life, there are instances where you will make accidental purchases. If you place an accidental order, or decide you don't need an item immediately after making the purchase, say the "wake word [your wake word], followed by "cancel order". If Alexa fails to cancel the order, use the Alexa app to follow the link in the order card to cancel your order.

What to Expect When Shopping With Alexa: Some Alexa Shopping Responses to Look Out For

When	Alexa's Response
When Alexa finds a previous order for an item you've asked her to shop for	If you **have a confirmation code** Alexa will say, "[item]. The order total is $[X]. To order, tell me your voice code If you **don't have a confirmation code**, Alexa will say, "[Item]. The order total is $[X]. Should I order it?"
Alexa fails to find a previous order and has to make recommendation from Amazon's Choice	"I didn't find that in your order history, but Amazon's Choice for [item] is [product name]. The order total is $[X]. Should I order it?"
When Alexa fails to find a previous order item and the item or a similar items are not recommended from Amazon's choice	"I didn't find that in your past orders, so I've added [item] to your Shopping list."

When An item no longer qualifies for Amazon prime	"I found [the name of the item] but can only reorder Prime-eligible products. Check your Alexa app for more options."
When an item is temporarily out of stock	"I found [the name of the item], but it's temporarily out of stock and should arrive around [the expected date when the item will be available]. The order total is $[The total amount]. Should I order it?"
When an item features prime shipping only as an add-on item or a prime pantry item	"I found [the name of the item], but cannot order Prime Pantry items/Add-on Items. Check your Alexa app for more options."
When you attempt to place an order without Prime membership	"I found [the name of the item], but can only re-order products for Prime members. Check your Alexa app for more options."

When you attempt to make an order but Alexa notices a problem with the 1-click billing address on your Amazon account	"Sorry, but there's a problem with the billing address on your account. Please visit Amazon.com to complete your order.

How to Upload Offline Music to Your Amazon Music Library and Play the Music on Your Echo Device

Load your own music to the Echo!

Amazon Echo does not accept or play music in CDs or other devices where you store your music, but it allows the user to upload as many songs as they need to the device and play them for free. Upload your favorite music to the Cloud music player for free and play it as much as you want.

Note: Surprisingly, because Echo works best with an active WiFi connection, you can't ask Echo to play music or audio files stored on your Amazon cloud drive. However, Alexa can play audio files stored on your Amazon Music library or your Audible files if the files are audiobooks.

Amazon Cloud player is an easy to use feature that will allow you to do this easily. Once you have uploaded your favorite music, command the device to play any song you love as much as you want, and its great quality speakers will make you enjoy the best quality music at all times.

Since you may not upload all your favorite songs at once, you can keep changing your favorite playlist in order to enjoy the best music every day. This ensures that you always have something great to listen from your Echo.

Whether you're a prime account holder or not, Amazon gives you a free music library. To access your music library, navigate to your account menu and select "Your Music Library" from the drop down menu. Your Amazon music Library can hold up to 250 songs without the need for a prime membership. Further, as an Amazon account holder, you also get free access to the Amazon Music Player for the web and mobile apps.

There are advantages to being a prime member. One of these is that with a prime Amazon account, you have unlimited access to the Prime Music Library and are free to grab songs, playlists, and albums and add them to your music library. Further, any music grabbed from the prime library does not affect the 250+ songs space offered by Amazon.

If you're a music enthusiast, you know that 250 songs is just a slice of the pie. If you have a large music library or aim to have on in the future, you can subscribe to the premium music library at a cost of $24.99/year and increase your music library space to 250,00 songs in your downloadable and playable library. 250,000 tracks are a massive space allocation.

For example, if you ripped hundreds of audio CDs and uploaded them to your account, the amounting tracks would probably not surpass the 250,000 songs limit. If you have an existing music library with another service such as ITunes or other media, you can port your music library into Amazon for use with Alexa and the Echo.

Note: To upload music to your Amazon music library may take some time and effort commitment especially if you own a large music library. Before you upload music into your Amazon music library, you need to get the music ready.

If your music library is on another cloud-based service such as iCloud, this means downloading each song, and recreating all your playlists from scratch. If your music library is CD form that means, you'll have to rip the music and tag your songs accordingly.

Note: If your music library is on another cloud-based service such as iCloud, you may have grown accustomed to having many customization options for your songs. For example, with iCloud, you can add notes to each track, rate each track individually, and create custom Metadata for your songs. This is not the case with Amazon music library. However, Amazon offers the following crucial customization options: Title, Artist, Album Artist, Album, Genre, and year as also shown in the figure below.

Edit Song Info

	Get Info from Amazon
Title:	Hollow Eyes
Artist:	Red Lorry Yellow Lorry
Album Artist:	Red Lorry Yellow Lorry
Album:	Talk About The Weather
Genre:	Rock
Year: 1985	Track: 4 Disc: 1

Help   Cancel   OK

After readying your music, the first thing you need to do is decide if you should have a prime account if you don't have one. The choice to upgrade to Music Premium Player will largely depend on the size of your music library. If your music library is larger than the 250 songs free space provided by Amazon, you will have to go the premium way. Again, there are tons of benefits to going premium. For example, if you have a large music library, you can use your Premium Music Library as an offsite music backup.

To upload your music once it's ready, navigate to your account tab on your Amazon account, and select "Your Music Library" you will be prompted to sign up for Amazon music account if you haven't.

The sign up process is relatively easy: just follow the prompts and complete signup. Once the signup is complete, on your left panel, you'll notice an "upload your music to your cloud library" option. Choose this option to upload offline music to your Cloud library.

Note: If you have a massive digital library with another service such as iCloud, to move this music into your Amazon Library and make it playable on the Echo, you need to download every song from your cloud library. If you have a huge library, this will take a take a lot of download time and an external space or hard drive big enough to house your library of songs. Further, because a massive download may lag internet speeds on other connected devices, you may need to segment your songs downloads.

As you download your library from another cloud-service, you should also make a point of downloading all additional files that may contain metadata, track titles, artist's names, album cover, etc. If you download the music from a service such as iTunes, you may also need to remove DRM (digital rights management) from your music. DRM is a feature that protects songs from unauthorized copying to other media libraries such as the Amazon cloud Player.

After you are done stripping digital rights management from your music (this is important especially to an iTunes library), the next thing you want to do is upload your now offline library into your Amazon music library.

How long uploading your music library takes will vary and largely depend on the size of your music library. If your library is massive, you can expect the upload to take long. There is no formula to the upload. All you need to do is go back into your Amazon account, click on "Your Music Library" and search for the "Upload Your Music" option as shown below

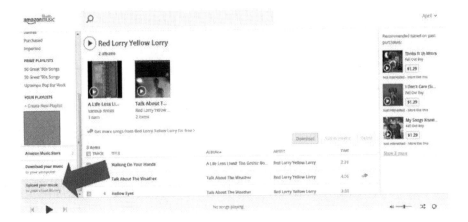

If this is your first time uploading anything to your music library, Amazon will prompt you to download the Amazon Music up-loader plugin/program or install the Adobe Flash player plugin. After downloading the up-loader, follow the simple self-explanatory prompts to upload your music library. Depending on the size of your music library, you may need to "choose files and folders" option to chunk-out your library upload.

After your music library uploads to Amazon music library, you may also want to check your music to ensure that all files are uploaded successfully and that there are no missing files (how long that takes will depend on the size of your music library). An important thing to not is that if your library is massive, missing songs will not be glaring. In this instance, it is best to keep an offline or online backup of your music to ensure that, if some songs are not available on your Amazon Music Library, you can skip back to your offline backup and upload missing songs to your music library for use with Alexa.

Enjoy New Prime Stations

Subscribers of prime stations can also get to enjoy different stations through their Amazon Echo, free of ads, and this means that you listen to pure music with no interruptions at all. Choose a station that you want to listen to, specify it with your voice command, and the device will play it for you. Vote for your favorite stations on Prime and your device will always remember what you like most. You can ask it to repeat the song for you, or to replay the song after some time, depending on what you like. Using Echo will be absolutely fun for music lovers. Echo's remote control can also allow you to select what you want to listen to with ease if you do not want to use your voice command.

To get you started, simply ask Alexa to play a specific Prime Station by its name e.g. you can say something like "Alexa, play 'Top Pop' Prime Station. And when it starts playing, you can go back, forward etc. You can even ask Alexa to give it a thumbs down or thumbs up to personalize the station a little bit. If you want to add a song to your music library, you can simply issue the following command when the song is playing "Alexa, add this song to my library".

With the Prime Stations, you can navigate your musical selections using voice requests. Try the following ideas:

- You can play a prime station by simply saying something like; "Alexa, play Katy Perry", or "Alexa, play the best of Prime Music playlist".

- You can control playback by saying "Alexa, next" or Alexa, go back" or Alexa, resume/pause."

- You can personalize your Prime Stations by simply asking such questions like "Alexa, thumbs down/thumbs up."

- You can ask Alexa what song is playing by simply asking "Alexa, what name is this?"

Listen to iHeart Radio Music

Amazon Echo is able to play iHeart radio music, free of ads for its users. If you have an iHeart account, just link it up to your device and enjoy great quality iHeart radio music at all times. You can always enjoy quality music according to your mood, favorite artists, or your favorite genre, and our device will always play it in the quality that you like the most. Here is how to connect iHeart Radio to Amazon Echo:

Open the left navigation panel from the Amazon Echo app then select **Settings>>Music services**. You should be able to see all the music services that are available on Amazon Echo. Select the link titled iHeartRadio to link your Echo with iHeart.

You can learn more about it here.

Note: The general (and fairly direct) way of streaming music on Echo is to use the following command to instruct Echo to stream your desired music:

"Alexa, play {number on the dial- on Amazon music services list} {station name}"

For instance, if you want to play a station on TuneIn, you can for instance say

"Alexa, play {number on the dial} {station name} on TuneIn"

Enjoy Your Favorite Pandora Radio Stations

The Echo and Alexa seem to be in consistent development mode. Every day, Amazon adds new features to the Eco making it better for its users. One of these features that Amazon has been very eager to add to the echo is Pandora. You can now connect your Pandora account to the Echo and use Alexa to play your favorite Pandora music.

Unfortunately, these will be played with ads, as well, but since it is great quality music at all times, you will definitely enjoy it all. If you have a Pandora account, link it up to your Amazon Echo app. Always specify whenever you are commanding your device to play an individual station from Pandora, and it shall be done as you command.

To do this, you need to download the Echo app if you don't already have it (if you don't have the app, it probably means you haven't setup your Echo. You should probably do so now using the instructions we looked at in an earlier chapter).

Once the app is on your smart device, fire it up and select the hamburger menu in the upper right corner. From the list, select Pandora and choose the "link your account now option".

Here, if you don't have an existing Pandora account, create one. If you have a Pandora account, choose "I have a Pandora account" to sign in with your registered Pandora email and password. Once you're done with this step, it will create an association between your Pandora account and your Echo app and display your station. To play a station on the Echo, simply select what you want to play on the Echo. With the app, you can control music playback, volume, switch between stations, create new stations, and view album arts. You can also say "Alexa Play Pandora" to get Alexa to play your

Pandora music. When you say this, Alexa will grab the station you last listened to and play it. If you're on a computer, you can also get the echo to play Pandora music through the Echo web Interface.

Note: Pandora is in the list of Amazon's music services so setting it up will be just the same as setting up iHeart stations.

Another way you can go about it is to set the Echo as a Bluetooth speaker. In this case, simply say "Alexa, pair Bluetooth". Alexa will then respond with the instructions you should follow to set up the Bluetooth settings on your tablet or phone. Once you've paired the two, any of the audio you have queued on your device will start playing through Echo.

Note: If you follow this option, all the controls (next, pause, play), will be done on your phone. This option works for all music services that are not on Amazon music services list shown <u>here</u> like Spotify and your personal music library or your audiobooks.

To listen to audiobooks on Kindle Unlimited or Audible, here is what to do:

You can say:

Alexa, play the book "Rich Dad Poor Dad"

Alexa, play the audiobook "Rich Dad Poor Dad"

Alexa, play "Rich Dad Poor Dad" from Audible

Alexa, read "Rich Dad Poor Dad"

Alexa, go back/forward (*this forwards or rewinds by 30seconds*)

Alexa, resume my book

Alexa, pause

Alexa, stop reading the book in 20 minutes

Alexa, set a sleep timer for 25minutes

Alexa, cancel sleep timer

Receive Accurate Weather Reports

Alexa will give you weather updates of a particular location that you may be interested in at any given time. It may not tell you how much it will snow for instance or how much it will rain, but you will definitely know that it will snow or rain in a certain area at a particular time or specific day. The device can also inform you how long the weather will be the way it is so that you can make the right decisions. If you are traveling, this information will be of great value to you. It is also the best device to help you plan your outdoor activities. So how can you receive such reports? Here is how:

Alexa usually uses <u>AccuWeather</u> to get the latest weather information. When you ask Alexa about the weather, you should see a card within the app that displays 7-day weather forecast for the requested location. Here is how to set it up:

Access the Alexa app and then visit the left navigation panel and then click on Settings then select your device.

Select Edit on the Device location section then key in the complete address of the location you want to get weather information including the street name, city, state and zip code then proceed to select Save.

Once you have that done, you can then command Alexa to tell you about various things about the weather. Here is how to go about it:

Say this (Always start with Alexa)	To do this
e.g. "Alexa, what's the weather"	To ask about the current weather in your selected location
Will it be windy tomorrow? Will it snow or rain tomorrow?	To ask about any harsh weather conditions in the selected location
What's the weather in {City, state, or city, country}?	To ask about the weather forecast in another city, besides the one you've selected
What's the weather for {day}? What's the weather for this week?	What's the weather for this weekend

Access Information Instantly

Amazon Echo is able to provide you with instant information, especially on the latest sports scores and updates. This will ensure that even though you may not be watching a game, you still know exactly what is happening. This does not apply to the sports that are being played only in your country; Alexa is able to connect to scores in a range of countries around the globe.

For instance, it is now possible for you to get schedules and scores for various NCAA FBS (Division 1-A) football games. You can as well get the same information for NHL, MLB, WNBA, MLS, NCAA men's basketball and NBA games. Additionally, it is possible for you to ask for scores of completed games or live scores or even find out when your favorite team is playing its next game. For instance, if you want to learn when Oregon Ducks is playing, simply ask "Alexa, when is the next Oregon Ducks game?"

You can as well set up a customized Sports Update to get information about your preferred teams. This feature allows you to know your favorite team's schedules and latest games. To set up the customization feature, simply open your Alexa App then select Sports Update from the Settings. You can then add your favorite teams. Once you are done, you can now simply ask Alexa "Alexa, give me my Sports Update"

Get Accurate Traffic Updates Any Time

Alex can also send you traffic reports once you set up traffic updates. The traffic updates are real time traffic data that offer you the shortest route to your destination of choice and the travel time it shall take to get to your destination. The weather update feature is especially useful if you commute to work or school daily.

You can always avoid the hassle of traffic using your Amazon Echo. Visit Echo.Amazon.com and enter your home and work address to always receive traffic updates in real time. Your device will give you a better alternative if the road you always use is jammed with traffic to allow you to get there on time.

How to Setup Traffic Reports on Amazon Echo

To use this feature, set up a commute route in your echo app. To do this, fire up your app, from the hamburger menu, go to settings and select traffic.

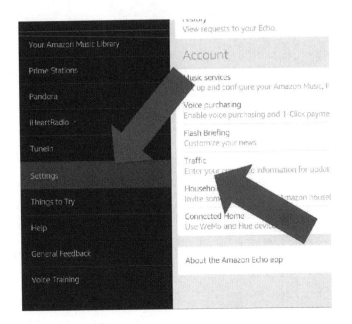

Your Amazon Music Library

Prime Stations

Pandora

iHeartRadio

TuneIn

Settings

Things to Try

Help

General Feedback

Voice Training

History
View requests to your Echo.

Account

Music services
up and configure your Amazon Music, F

Voice purchasing
Enable voice purchasing and 1-Click payme

Flash Briefing
Customize your news

Traffic
Enter your   e information for updat

Household
Invite som   Amazon housel

Connected Home
Use WeMo and Hue devic

About the Amazon Echo app

When you select this option, set up your start, stop, and end-points. To this end, the app will triangulate the Echo's location and use that location as the starting point. You can change this by clicking on the "change address link" on the far right of your current location.

If your route has stops along the way, click on the "new stop link" option to add multiple stops. Make sure that each stop has a street address. At the bottom, you shall see an "add address option link". Use this to enter your end-point making sure to give it a street address.

If you have no specific street address in mind and simply need to know the traffic in a general location, attraction, or city, Google search the street address for a shop, eatery, or business in the vicinity of the area you intend to get traffic updates from and use that as your end point.

Once that is setup, you can get Alexa to give you traffic reports and provide you the fastest route to your destination by asking her the following:

"Alexa, traffic report"

"Alexa, how's traffic?"

"Alexa, how's my commute?"

The Echo prides itself in adaptability. When it comes to weather reports, it does not disappoint. You can use the Echo to set up multiple commutes. For example, if a member of your household has an Amazon account, the Echo can store a separate commute for its traffic report functionality. To set up another commute, you need to set up Amazon Household.

Create and Manage Your Shopping List with Ease

You do not have to create a shopping list the hard way, like writing everything out, when you have the Amazon Echo. Add items to your shopping list with convenience as you remember them. Once the list is full and you are ready to go shopping, either command it to print the list for you, or have it transfer the list to your mobile phone, so that you can access it with ease as you shop.

Your Amazon Echo can also shop for you! Just let it know what you are in need of and the device will order it for you. If you are an extremely busy person, you will enjoy this device so much. Here is how to make this possible:

When you visit Amazon.com (you should be signed in to your account), you should see a link to your Alexa Shopping list on the homepage and within the Wish List menu. You can click here to go to the Alexa Shopping List.

Tip: You can use this <u>IFTTT recipe</u> to get an email of everything on your shopping list. And if you prefer to get the shopping list on Evernote, you can use this <u>IFTTT recipe</u>.

To make this part easy to understand for you, it is perhaps important that I explain more about managing lists using Amazon Echo:

Note: Some of the settings here may only be available through the Alexa app but you can bet that you should be able to use voice command for many of the actions.

When you open your Alexa app, you should see a timeline of your activity. There are "Cards" on the Home screen, which show a description of all your requests and usually have such features as:

- The option to remove the card

- An option to give feedback about your most recent interaction

- Various links to the web where you can get more information

- An option for you to search or browse related content within the Alexa app

- A detailed description of your most recent requests

From then on, you can use the app as explained below to achieve various goals:

Try this	To do this
From the left navigation panel, select "home"	This allows you to see a timeline of your activity and even get some more information regarding

	your request
Select an audio service right from the left navigation panel to help you search for content. Go to "now playing" to enable you to see the station art, album, a history of your tracks and your queue.	This allows you to search for various audio libraries and even listen to programs, stations, audiobooks, and music. You can click here to learn more about the basic commands relating to music.
Go to "to-do list" or "shopping list" from the navigation panel on the left	To manage your lists. Click here to learn for more information on how to manage your shopping list.
From the left navigation panel, select "Alarm" then select "Off" to disable an alarm	This makes it possible to manage an alarm. There is more information about managing alarms here.
From the left navigation panel, select "timer" then go to "cancel" to allow you to disable a timer	This makes it possible to cancel or pause a timer.
Set up and then configure the settings for your device	This one allows you to adjust your device settings

Listening to Music On Amazon Echo

Basic Music commands

Important note: If your music library doesn't have your genre, album, playlist, artist or song, Alexa will search the prime music catalogue or samples from your digital music store if available.

Here are some basic music commands that you should try:

Say this	To do this
Turn down/up the volume or turn the volume down/up Set the volume to level {number}	Adjust the volume
Who/what is this?	To hear the details of the track that is playing currently
Pause/stop	To stop/pause the track which is currently playing
Play/resume	To play tracks or songs
Next/previous track	To go to the next or previous track or to play or restart the song or track.
Loop	To loop the play queue when it is complete
Cancel sleep timer Stop playing music in {X} hours/minutes Set the sleep timer for {X}	This helps to set or cancel a sleep timer

minutes or hours	
Repeat Stop shuffle Shuffle	To shuffle tracks or songs

Note: Some features may not be supported on TunIn, iHeartRadio, Pandora and Prime Stations.

Here are some more advanced music commands

Say this	To make Alexa do this
Play the album/song {the name of the album/{the name of the song}}	This allows you to play specific album or song.
Listen to my {playlist name} playlist Shuffle my {the name of the playlist} playlist	This allows you to listen to a playlist
Play some {genre} music Play some {the name of the genre} music from Prime	This allows you to play music in a certain genre
Play songs by {the name of the artist}	This allows you to play a song by a certain artist
Play {the station frequency}	This allows you to play a radio station (iHeartRadio

Play the station {the name of the station} Play the station {the station call sign}	and TuneIn.
Play my {name of the artist} station on iHeartRadio/Pandora/Prime Music	This gets you to play a custom artist station
Play my {name of genre} station on iHeartRadio/Pandora/Prime Music	This gets you to play a custom genre station
Thumbs down/up I don't like this song/I like this song	This lets you like or dislike a song on Pandora, iHeartRadio and Prime Stations
Play {the name of the station from Prime Play {the name of the station} Prime Station.	This allows you to play a prime station.
Skip	This allows you to skip to the next song Important note: If you have a free Pandora account, you can only skip 6 times per hour per station. The same applies to iHeartRadio accounts but these allow up to 15 skips per day across all

	the Custom stations. You can skip unlimited times on Prime Stations
I am tired of this song	This will remove a song that is played frequently from the rotation (this works for Prime and Pandora Stations).
Create a Pandora, iHeartRadio based station based on {the name of the artist} Make a station for {artist}	

Working with alarms

Use the Alexa app	Say this
You can set new alarms using your voice. But if you want to edit alarm, you have to use the app.	In order to set an alarm, you can say the following: Set an alarm for {the time} Wake me up at {the time} Set the alarm for {the duration} from now
You cannot do this on the app	To snooze an alarm, say this: When the alarm is sounding, simply say, "Snooze" to snooze

	the alarm for 9 minutes.
On the left navigation panel, choose "alarm" then select the device and then view the alarms then turn them off or on	To check the status of your alarms, simply say: What time is my alarm set for? Important note: If you have several alarms that have been set, Alexa will simply read several of them and then direct you on how to check the rest within the app.
On the left navigation panel, select "alarm" then select your device and then proceed to select the alarm that you want to cancel then choose "off"	To cancel or stop an alarm simply say "stop alarm" (as the alarm is sounding). Or cancel alarm for {the period}. This cancels the alarm but doesn't delete it.
On the left navigation panel, select "alarm" then select your device and then select the alarm that you want to delete then choose "delete alarm".	You have to use the Alexa app
On the left navigation panel, go to "settings" then select your device and then choose "sounds". Proceed to press and then draw the volume bar for	You will need to use the Alexa app

"alarm and timer volume" Important: This doesn't change the overall volume of the device.	
On the left navigation panel, choose "settings" then select your device and then choose "sounds". You should then select Alarm default sounds, then pick a new sound. Note: This doesn't change the sound of your existing alarms. If you want to change that, follow the steps below: For a single alarm: On the left navigation panel, go to alarm Then choose your device and then select the alarm that you wanted to change. Then choose "alarm sound" and then select a new sound. Go back to the alarm screen and then choose "save changes"	This has to be done in the Alexa app.

Add a User from your Household to Your Device

✓   Make sure the family member you add is present.

✓   Select "Settings" from the left navigation panel in the Alexa app.

✓   Under account select "Manage your Amazon Household."

✓   Follow these same instructions to add a second family member to your Amazon household. During this process give your phone, laptop or tablet to the second person so they can add their account information.

Remove a user from your Household

✓   In the Alexa app selects settings in the left navigation.

✓   Under account select "Manage your Amazon Household."

✓   Now select "Remove" next to the person you want to remove.

✓   To remove, select "Leave".

✓   Switch to Another Profile after you Set Up your Household

✓   After you set up a Household, you can switch accounts between users on an Alexa device.

✓   Say, "Switch accounts."

You Will Love Home Automation Services

Amazon Echo has the ability to control various devices like switches and lights from SmartThings, Philips Hue, WeMo, Wink and Insteon by simply using your voice.

Important note: Amazon Fire TV is only compatible with the devices that use any hub service as shown below:

Hubs

Some of the devices connected to your home may require that you connect to a hub service to enable you to use Alexa to control them using your voice. Some of these include:

- ✓   Insteon

- ✓   SmartThings

- ✓   Wink

Note: Before connecting to any home device, ensure to read <u>Amazon Echo's Safety Information for using connected home devices with Alexa</u>.

Before getting started, ensure to go to the app store on your mobile device then download the manufacturer's companion app for the device you want to connect. Then set up and connect the hub and any compatible connected home devices within the same Wi-Fi network as the Alexa device. Then download and install the most recent software updates for the devices in question.

Now you can connect a hub service to Alexa by following the steps below:

Under the Alexa app, go to Settings then select "connected home" then under the "device links", choose the "link with {service}" option. You will see a third party login popping up in the app. Proceed to sign in with the third party information and follow the prompts until you complete setup. After you've connected the hub service, you can now add the connected home devices to your Alexa device by following the steps below:

Follow the prompts for **"before you begin"** for the hub service as explained above.

Then say the words "discover my devices" to find your devices. You can as well use the app then choose the "discover devices" option to find the devices. Alexa will confirm the start of the search. Then after finding the devices, you should hear

"Discovery is complete, in total, you have ### reachable connected under this device"

If Alexa finds the connected home devices. And if Alexa doesn't find the device(s), you will hear "discovery is complete. I couldn't find any devices".

If your device was found and connected to, you should now be in a position to control the device using your voice. And if your device is not reachable, you should see "unreachable" just next to the device within the app.

Important note: It may often take some time if you turn your connected home device off or unplug it and then turn it back on. And if Alexa does not discover the device, try checking the companion app to ensure that it is properly connected and that it is on the same Wi-Fi network as the Alexa device.

Note: The device groups that you often create within the manufacturer's companion app often show up in as individual (separate) devices within the Alexa app. Through the device group, it is possible to control multiple connected home devices at the same time using Amazon Echo. For instance, you can say such words like "Turn on Living room lights" or Set Bedroom lights to 20%. Here is how to create a device group:

Within the Alexa app, go to the left navigation panel and then choose "settings>>connected home. And then under the "Groups" category, choose "create group". Enter in the name of your group within the provided text field.

Note: Ensure to give your group a name that's easy for Alexa to recognize. For instance, try aiming for names with 2-3 syllables. And if you have multiple groups, try creating a new name for each group. For instance, you can set groups such as "bedroom", "living room", "verandah", basement etc.

Proceed to choose the connected home device(s) that you want to add to a particular group then choose "add". If you want to edit a connected home device group, follow the prompts below:

Select the connected home group under "groups" then proceed to make the necessary changes to the group then edit its name and then select the text field and then update the existing name.

You can add or remove any connected devices by simply selecting the checkboxes that are located right next to each device. And if you want to delete a group, simply select "Delete".

With what we've set up above, you should be able to control devices like switches and lights. Here is how to go about it:

Say this (always ensure to start with the wake word e.g. Alexa)	To do this
Set brightness to ###% Dim lights to ###%	This makes it possible to set the brightness of different compatible devices
Turn off/on {connected home	Turn on/off the connected

device home} e.g. Turn off/on thermostat	home devices

You can adjust the color of Philips Hue bulbs by using the Philips Hue app.

Devices

You can use the following compatible manufacturers' devices to set the brightness of compatible devices.

- ✓ Philips Hue

- ✓ Insteon

- ✓ SmartThings

- ✓ Wink

Let's take a quick look at how these work:

Echo & WeMo

Alexa can control some of the home appliances that you have connected to a WeMo control device. You can, for instance, connect your air conditioner to your Echo to always command it to turn on or off without physically getting involved. Have it discover your appliances to get started, and it will always control them for you. Echo works with WeMo Switch, WeMo Insight Switch, and WeMo Light switch to fully take control of home appliances.

Alexa can also control your Philips bulbs. It works very well with some of the standard Philips bulbs we have today, for instance, Phillips BR 30 bulb, Phillips Light Strip, Phillips Bloom light and so many others.

For you to get started with this, simply connect Your Hue and WeMo devices to your home Wi-Fi then name each device in its respective app. When you are fully set up, simply say "Alexa, discover my appliances". Alexa will confirm your command then allow you to control these devices.

With this option, you can try out the following commands:

✓ Alexa, turn off the coffee maker

✓ Alexa, turn on the fan

✓ Alexa, turn off the living room fan

✓ Alexa, turn off the hallway light

You can even get a lot more creative by using IFTTT automated recipes such as:

✓ Scheduling to switch on the porch lights when you are about to get home or switching them off when you close the front door etc.

✓ You can also use the Long Press to control the lights without using the app.

✓ Besides that, you can create many more conditional relationships between various products then connect them to different online apps.

You can check some of the IFTTT recipes you can use <u>here</u> to make your life easier.

Wink

The collaboration between the Amazon Echo and Wink results in an excellent smart lighting control to the home or office. There is a range of products which are compatible with Wink, and these include lighting products from Lutron, General Electric and Leviton. Now, Alexa is able to control these products. There products include plug-in switches and lights.

Soon, through Wink, it will be possible for the Echo to connect to the lock of doors, which can be especially helpful for anyone looking to quickly open their garage doors or heighten their security. The main advantage of the collaboration between Wink and Amazon Echo is that it works towards creating a smarter home in the near future.

To integrate Wink with Amazon Echo, ensure to have connected your Echo to the Wink Hub by following the above instructions. Once you have your Wink hub connected, go to your Amazon account in the Echo app then click on Settings then scroll down until you get to the "connected home" tab. Then from there, you can choose "link with Wink devices" from where you will be required to sign in to your Wink account.

Note: You can learn more about it <u>here</u>.

SmartThings

SmartThings is compatible with the Amazon Echo, which makes it easy to control the lights and switches that are compatible with SmartThings, as well as any product that is able to be plugged in to a power outlet for SmartThings. What is brilliant about this integration is that as the SmartThings Hub updates, the Amazon Echo will update as well, allowing for the Echo to be used here in the considerable future.

Note: Linking SmartThings with Amazon Echo follows the same formula as in Wink or any other hub that we've discussed above.

LIFX Bulbs & Amazon Echo

How To Connect LIFX Bulbs To The Echo And Use Alexa To Control Them

Since its release, the Echo has found many uses in the home. With its IFTTT ability, you can control smart devices around the home (we looked at some of these devices earlier). One of these devices is the LIFX line of bulbs. When you connect your Echo to your line of LIFX bulbs, you can command Alexa to turn your LIFX bulbs on or off, increase or decrease brightness, and change the bulbs color.

Unfortunately, setting up your LIFX bulbs to work with the Echo and Alexa can present a challenge especially since to get the two optimally integrated, you have to group your LIFX bulbs to create themes.

To get started, the first thing you want to do is to de-box your bulbs, fix them onto their fixtures, and turn them on. The types of bulb and bulb fixture you use have will vary from home to home. For example, you can choose to use First-Gen standard 120V LIFX bulbs on standard lamp fixtures or you may use the newer 100 series LIFX bulbs on standard lamp fixtures. It is very important to ensure that your light fixture and your LIFX bulb are compatible.

Once you've fixed your lamps to their fixtures, the next thing you need to do is install the latest version of the LIFX app to your primary Smart device. The app is available for Android and IOS. After installing the app, fire it up and follow through the prompts to get started. After the get started screen, you should see the "add your bulb" screen.

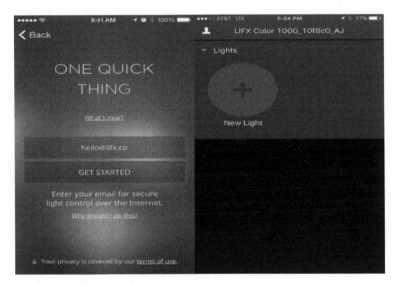

When you press the 'new light' option, the app will search the near vicinity for all LIFX bulbs and list them. If you encounter problems and the app fails to find LIFX bulbs within the vicinity and populate a list, do the following.

On your smart device, press the home button and navigate to settings, select WIFI options, and select the LIFX bulb network. If your LIFX network bears the name LIFX Bulb, your password is lifx1234, enter it when prompted for a password (note: this step may be unnecessary for newer version of LIFX bulbs). When you connect to this network, switch back to the LIFX app if the app does not pop up a dropdown window asking you to head back into the app. The app should at this point list all available LIFX bulbs available in the vicinity.

Select and add each bulb to your network individually by finding your preferred network, select connect bulb and enter your WIFI password when the app prompts you. Repeat this step with all LIFX bulbs you want to add to your network. The app will place all your available bulbs to the List screen and in the default group of lights also available in the list screen.

On the list screen, if a bulb is on, you can use the colored circles around each bulb to know that particular bulb's color and level of brightness. On the other hand, if the bulb is off, the ring and bulb icon will be grayed off.

To view a particular bulb and its details, tap the bulb's name. To adjust the color of your bulbs, select a color from the color wheel (Note: the arrow at the top indicates the currently selected color). To adjust the brightness, drag up and down at the middle of the circle. Use the icons at the bottom to shift between colors and whites, or use the effects option to set special effects such as color cycling and candle light (this will happen on another screen).

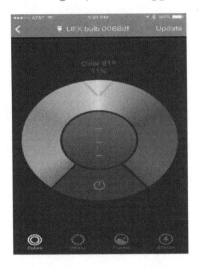

Once the bulbs are all set up, you may also want to update each bulb individually. The update link should be at the upper right corner of that bulb's details. When you tap on it, it shall prompt a firmware update. Note: Depending on your Internet connection, the update may take up to 30 minutes.

After updating all your bulbs and making sure they are all turned on (not grayed off in the app), the next step involves connecting your Echo. To do that, you need to claim your bulbs from the LIFX cloud. Without this step, your echo, which connects to the LIFX cloud to control your bulbs, will not integrate well.

To claim your bulb, look at individual bulb details. Where once there was an update link (before you updated your bulbs firmware), there should be a claim link. When you claim your first bulb, you'll have to create a password for the LIFX cloud account. Once you create a password, claim all your LIFX bulbs.

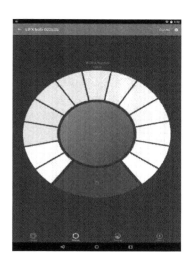

The LIFX app gives you the option to rename each bulb to a name of your choice and group them into different groups. For example, if you have 2 bulbs in the kitchen, 2 in the office, and 2 in the living room, you can rename these into Kitchen 1, Kitchen 2, Office 1, Office 2, Living Room 1, and Living Room 2, and group them by room.

To rename your bulbs, go into the details of a particular bulb. On the upper right hand corner, they'll be a pencil icon where the claim and update link previously were. If there is no pencil, to bring up the bulb editable details, tap and hold on bulb's name. Don't be afraid to experiment with the bulbs colors to get them to your liking. Once you get ach bulb to be exactly how it, rename each bulb appropriately.

Note: Grouping your bulbs will make it easier to control groups of bulbs by using Alexa.

After getting your bulbs exactly how you want them (including the names and groupings), navigate into the Alexa app and enable LIFX skill. Here, you will be prompted to enter your LIFX cloud account details to log in to your account and connect your echo to your LIFX cloud. Use the Alexa app to sample the Interaction phase and substitute the existing bulbs with your won bulbs and bulb groups.

When you're all done with this setup, you will have no use for switches when controlling your LIFX bulbs and bulbs groups. You can use Alexa to control the bulbs (you'll have to leave them powered on at all times for this to work). You can also use the LIFX app to turn your bulbs on and off randomly (vacation mode)

Note: When issuing voice commands to Alexa to control your bulbs LIFX is pronounced as Life Ex. For example, to command Alexa to control LIFX bulbs in the kitchen, you can use a group name to give Alexa the command "Alexa, tell Life Ex to change my kitchen lights to yellow."

Access Wikipedia Articles through Voice command

Any information that you may need from Wikipedia can be accessed with just a voice command to Alexa. Ask Alexa the age of an individual celebrity you are following for instance; ask her the definition of certain terminologies for your homework; ask any information pertaining to a matter that you need in detail. There are a lot that you can learn every day if you make good use of your Amazon Echo. So how can you use this feature? Here is how to make this work:

{Wake word}, Wikipedia, {keyword or phrase}

e.g. "*Alexa, Wikipedia, Facebook*". This will give the information about Facebook which is available on Wikipedia.

Use Amazon from Different Accounts

If there are two of you, for example, in a household, you do not each need to get your own Amazon Echo, you can both use the same one with ease. To begin with, you may choose to link up the families' Prime accounts to your Amazon Echo.

All that you need to do is visit the website www.echo.amazon.com, and find and select **Settings** on the left navigation panel. Then, find the option to **set your household profile** up and follow the instructions. Preferably, the members of your household should be Prime members.

Tip: Follow the above instructions for any subsequent profile that you want to add to your Amazon household. You will need to pass the phone, tablet, or PC to the next person to set up their account information.

Once you have linked them, your family members have to use their mobile devices to download the Amazon Echo app, and then select the option to become a part of the household.

Once this is done, it is possible to get access to information that is on the account of someone in your household, such as music playlists.

When someone becomes a member of the household, they create a profile. To access that profile, you may need to ask your Echo to let you know the profile that you are using at that moment. Simply ask *"Alexa, which account is this?"*

If it is not the one that you want to use, ask Alexa to switch profiles (by stating the name of the profile that you want to switch to), and your Echo will do so; thus, giving you access to what is in that Amazon account. Simply say something like *"Alexa, Switch*

Accounts". As you browse a content library within the Alexa app, try to use the dropdown menu at the very top of the screen to toggle between multiple user libraries.

To remove a user from your household, simply select Settings on the left navigation panel of the Alexa app then under "Account", select on "Manage your Amazon Household" then select "remove" just next to the person that you want to remove. If you want to remove yourself, you can simply select "leave" then select "remove from Household" to confirm the change.

Note 1: After adding a second adult to your household, this simply means that you are essentially authorizing them to use any credit cards that are associated with your Amazon account for any purchases on Amazon. You will need a 4-digit code that you will say aloud whenever you want to confirm purchases with your credit card. If you want to confirm using a confirmation code, simply select "settings" within the Alexa app then select on Voice Purchasing.

Note 2: After removing a user from a household, keep in mind that you won't be able to add both user accounts to any other household for about 180 days. But if you remove someone by accident and want to add them back to your household, simply contact Customer Support to get help.

Keep All Your Information Up To Date

As your Amazon Echo is a digitized device which includes a CPU within, it uses software for its operations which needs to be updated often so that you are able to enjoy all of its latest features.

Normally, the device will look for updates each evening, though there might be an instance when you prefer to have an update before the end of the day.

If this is the case, first press the mute button. After this, leave the device to stay muted for no less than 30 minutes. When you take the device off mute, you will find that you have executed an early update.

Productive Things to do with your Amazon Echo

It is now clear that Amazon Echo is much more than a speaker and an assistant. You can use it for your own entertainment as well, to add convenience into literally every aspect of your life. However, you can also use the Amazon Echo to help you become more productive. This way, this amazing device is not only something that you speak to for various functions, it is also a tool that will help you to drastically improve every area of your life.

For this to occur with incredible ease and increased efficiency, Amazon has created the Alexa Fund. This fund is an investment firm for Amazon's developers. Through it, developers in any area are able to receive funding should they come up with an idea that is innovative using voice technology. Developers would need to come up with new capabilities for Alexa to make the Echo more productive. They can also choose to build up devices that are able to utilize Alexa by utilizing the Alexa Voice Service (AVS), as well as the Alexa Skills Kit (ASK). As it stands, there is up to $100 million that has been set aside to drive technology forward using Alexa.

The Alexa Voice Service can be used to develop any connected device, which includes a speaker, as well as a microphone for the purpose of incorporating voice enabled functions. It works this way when you speak to Alexa using a microphone on the device; she is able to respond through its speakers. Having this capability makes your product more cutting edge and competitive in the market.

When you have a device that is using the Alexa Voice Service, the hardware that it uses will enjoy extended capabilities. This has meaning for the customers who shall be using the device. To begin with, rather than requiring an app to give a command, it is possible to speak to the microphone so that the demand can be executed. This, in turn, makes customer interaction more natural.

Furthermore, there is no need of having an infrastructure to use AVS as it is based on a cloud and therefore, can reach a large scale. This adds to the aspect of lower costs as an advantage, especially when you consider that you can use AVS to create voice enabled experiences for your devices at no cost.

Using the AVS and ASK together helps to create an excellent experience and improves the interaction that a person can experience with their product. To get started, the only requirements that you need are a speaker and microphone as well as an internet connection.

Here are several ways that you can get Alexa to help you become more productive:

Make the Most of Third Party Skills

There are more third party skills being added to Alexa to make her much more useful. With more developers using the Alexa Skills Kit (ASK), the new voice drive capabilities for Alexa are impressive. Here are some of that you can experience:

✓ *StubHub*

This is one of the Third Party Skills that can help someone save time when looking for information on entertainment events. By entering your chosen city, you can find out what is happening in that city during the day and night, or even on a particular date. You can also discover what is happening in other cities. Therefore, when you are planning your next visit, you ensure that you pick the right date, time and place for the best effect or desired result.

For instance, if your city is New York, you can say something like "Alexa, ask StubHub what will be happening this weekend" to get her to tell you lots of stuff that are happening near your selected city (you will need to set up your city). You can also ask Alexa what's happening in other cities. To do that, start by saying "Alexa, launch StubHub". You will be guided through the entire process. E.g. After launching, Alexa will ask you how she can help, then you can say something like "what's happening in DC on Friday?"

You can as well change your home city by saying something like "Alexa, ask StubHub to change my home location"

✓   *Bart Times*

This skill can help you plan and organize your day as it provides you with the times for BART trains. For this to work, you need to begin by setting both your home station and your destination station. This can be done easily with a voice command such as, 'Alexa, set my home station.' From here, you can get the times for the next trains, and find out if their advisories are working well. Over time, the skill will begin to understand your personal settings, and getting the information that you need will become much faster and easier.

✓   *Math Puzzles*

What better way to keep your mind active than to find ways in which you can actively exercise it? Math Puzzles are one of the Third Party Skills that you can enjoy on your Amazon Echo. This is because it lets you challenge yourself by asking certain math questions and allowing you some time to answer the question. You can also challenge your friends with similar questions and you will discover who was able to answer the questions faster. It also prompts you to make a guess as to what the following number in a sequence may be.

✓   *Word Master*

This is another skill that is targeted towards improving the way that you think and the sharpness of your mind. It helps you to challenge yourself using words. To begin, Alexa will say one word. Then, you need to reply to Alexa with a word that begins with the last letter of the word that Alexa said. Once you say your word, Alexa then responds to your word in the same way. With each word, you earn a score, and as the word gets longer, your score gets higher. You can enjoy healthy competition with Alexa, all while giving your brain an amazing workout. When either you or Alexa fails to come up with a word, it's game over.

✓   *Trove*

This skill will provide you with the latest headlines from any topic that you seek. When you ask Alexa for that topic, it will find the top five headlines that relate to it. This way, you can easily later research for more direct information, and you can have an overview of what is happening in a particular area.

✓   *Focus Word*

Starting your day centered and focused may be exactly what you need to ensure that your day is productive and has the desired impact that you seek. This skill can help you create a day that is more productive as it offers you a word or phrase that is inspirational, and on which you can meditate. It has a good dose of humor as well as inspiration. So, in addition to giving you added insight, you will also end up with a smile on your face.

Note: For the Skills mentioned above, you can simply enable them on your Echo Smarthome app. On the app, simply tap on "Skills" in the menu and then select "Enable" to make that skill available for use.

Note: There are more skills in a subsequent chapter focused on fun things you can do.

Knowledge Management

Being productive requires you to find ways in which you can manage your knowledge and the information that is out there. On your mobile devices or laptops, you may be using folders and files to save your information for later reference. This makes it easier to find when you need to refer to it next. The Amazon Echo may not be a storage device, but it does have many advantages for those who require knowledge management.

What the Amazon Echo does is help you eliminate steps in a task that you are working on by cutting out a large number of unnecessary steps. For example, you need to get some information in the morning; this could include the news headlines, traffic updates, address book and calendar plan for the day, and information on the weather. While you prepare for your day, you can simply ask Alexa for this information, and without having to swipe a mobile device or pick up a newspaper, you will get all that you need. This allows you to free up your time to gather information that will be much more important for you.

Sync Your Calendars

You do not need to create a special calendar just to get the information that you need from your Amazon Echo. You can simply share your Google Calendar with your Amazon Echo, allowing you to quickly get the information that you need at your convenience. All that is required is for you to input the details of your Google Calendar into the Alexa app, and you can get your schedule with ease.

How to Add Your Google Calendar to Echo

Step #1

Open the Echo app on your phone or tablet.

Step #2

Tap on the bars on the top left. Now you have come to the "settings" bar. Now tap on it.

Step#3

Tap on "Calendar Services."

Step #4

Tap on "link accounts to Google." Enter your Google password on the next page.

Step#5

If you see your name on the "Calendar Services" you are now setup. Your Google calendar is set up in your Echo device. If you want to unlink your calendar tap on the "Unlink Google account" link. This link will be found directly under your name.

How to Connect Your Google Calendar to Amazon Echo

Connecting Google calendar is another new feature recently added to the echo feature's plate. Let us take a brief look at how you can do this.

Step #1

Launch the Echo app and navigate to setting and on to calendar services, and select 'link Google calendar account'

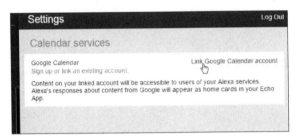

After clicking on the link indicated above, you need to sign in with your Google account credentials and follow the prompts to allow Echo access to your Google account and in extension, calendar.

After going through the verification process, you can use different voice commands to get Alexa to tell you what is in your Google calendar.

For example, you can ask Alexa the following

- "Alexa, what's on my calendar"

- "Alexa, what's on my calendar Monday?"

- "Alexa, when is my next event?"

- "Alexa, what's on my calendar tomorrow at 10 p.m.?"

As a point of note, you should know that Echo will only work with your calendar and not shared calendars. You can also use Alexa to create events on your Google calendar. Moreover, when you add new schedules to your calendar during your workday, Alexa will know and can read this to you on command at home.

Set Up an Automatic Kitchen Timer

Using the Amazon Echo, you can take a few steps closer to being a Master Chef. That is because this device can easily be used as a kitchen timer, making it easy for you to keep track of what you are preparing whilst you are in the kitchen. This functionality is also ideal for any situation where you may need to keep track of time. For productivity, having this device to speak your command to ensure that your hands are free to carry out others tasks. Giving Alexa your command is much faster and easier than trying to use the timer that may be on your smart device or watch.

Here are some few commands you can use with Amazon Echo to set timers:

Use the Alexa app	To do this, say this
Use your voice to set timers	Set a countdown timer "Set a timer for {the amount of time}" "Set the timer for {the time}"

	Note: It is possible to set a countdown timer for up to 24hours.
Go to "timer" from the left navigation panel then choose your device and then select "edit" right next to the timer that you want to pause and then choose "pause"	To resume or pause the timer
To check the time that's remaining on a countdown On the left navigation panel, select "timer then choose your device and view the status of the timers.	To ask how much time is left on your next upcoming timers, simply say "how much time is left on my timer" Note: In you have a number of timers, you can use the Alexa app to manage them well.
Simply go to the left navigation panel and select "Timer". Then select your device and select "edit", which is right next to the timer that you want to stop then choose "cancel"	When the timer is sounding, you can say "stop the timer" or if you have an upcoming timer, you can say "cancel the timer for {the amount of time} Note: if you have several timers set at the same time, use the app for that.
From the left navigation panel, go to settings then select your device and then select "sounds".	You will need to change the countdown timer using the Alexa

Proceed to press and then drag the volume bar for the Timer and Alarm volume. Note: the volume for the alarm is usually independent from the overall volume	App

Fun Things That You Can Do With Your Amazon Echo

There are more and more skills that are being developed for the Amazon Echo, which makes it a device that offers more fun. As it is, you have noted some of the funny questions that you can ask Alexa if you want to be entertained. In addition to these, there are skills that you can try out that are fun. As more skills are being developed, here are some that you should try out.

High Low Guessing Game

This game can be great fun, because it works two ways. You could ask Alexa to choose a number, usually between 1 and 100. When she does, you need to try to guess what number she chose. Unless you give her the right answer, when you tell her the number in the opposing scenario, you could choose a number and then get Alexa to try to guess what it could be. On average, a game lasts around 7 turns.

Crystal Ball

Wondering what is going to happen to you tomorrow? If you are, then this might just be the skill that you need in order to set your mind at ease. It is meant to help one make a prediction on the future, much in the same way as a magic 8 ball or tarot cards. To get answers, make sure that the questions you ask or yes or no type questions.

For this skill, you can choose to launch the skill and then proceed to listen to the welcome message and then respond appropriately to the commands. Another option is to launch the skill and then issue a command all at once. Here is an illustration on how to command the Crystal Ball.

{Wake word}, ask Crystal Ball if I will win the lottery

{Wake word}, launch Crystal Ball and tell it I am ready

{Wake word}, ask Crystal Ball for my fortune

Cat Facts

Cat lovers will love this new skill from Alexa as it allows for you to find out about facts on everything to do with cats, including their behavior, anatomy and history. With this information, you will be able to better care for your beloved pet.

To open Cat Facts, simply say "{The wake word}, open Cat Facts"

This immediately gets Alexa to fetch and read a catch fact.

Alexa, where do you live?

Alexa, do you love me?

Alexa, Knock Knock?

Alexa, Tea. Earl Grey. Hot.

Alexa, what is your favorite color?

Alexa, How old are you?

Alexa, tell me a story.

Alexa, How should I get rid of a dead body?

Alexa, Will you marry me?

Alexa, do you know the muffin man?

Alexa, who are you?

Alexa, Is Siri your friend?

Alexa, are you spying on me?

Play a Prank

Asking these questions can be fun, especially as Alexa has a wacky sense of humor. However, you can go a little further and use Alexa to play a prank on the people within your house. For this prank, you will need to have a remote control (so that the people you are pranking would find it difficult to figure out that it is all you). Here is what you should do.

With your Amazon Echo in one room, go into another room. You will need to be able to speak directly into your Echo using the remote control. Get Alexa to say anything that you want by using the command, Alexa, Simon says ……..and then the statement that you want Alexa to say. Alexa will repeat exactly what you say, and the people in the other room will believe that the Echo is talking to them directly. It is hilarious watching them have this interesting experience, and can be an absolute blast if you do this with children.

Spending time with Alexa can become serious, especially if you are using her as your assistant and source of information. Taking a few moments aside for some light-hearted fun will help you better appreciate all that this device has to offer you.

How to Build a Trivia Skill in Less Than an Hour
Create an AWS account

✓   Search for the AWS Amazon site so you can open an account. When you locate the site, tap on "Create an AWS account." (You will need a credit card, but it is a free tier.)

✓   Just follow the online instructions. Don't worry about the IAM role because that will be taken care of later.

✓   You will have to receive a phone call and enter a pin number on your phone keypad.

✓   You are ready to sign up to your console. (It may take a long time for your AWS account to go live. You will be notified by e-mail when it does.)

✓   Set up a Lambda function

✓   Choose U.S East (N. Virginia) region (upper right) - this is the only region with free Alexa/ Lambda tier service.

✓   Choose Lambda from computing services (upper left). Don't "select blueprint."

✓   You are now in "Configure Function."

✓   Enter the name/description/runtime.

✓   Choose "entry code type" for "Edit Code inline" and copy and paste the node JavaScript you downloaded earlier.

✓   Set the handler and role like this:

✓   Keep handler as index.handler.

✓   Compile a new role lambda_ basic_ execution (see IAM role in the next step.) Also, if you have already used

Lambda, you could have a lambda_ basic_ execution already made for you that you can use.

✓ You will be prompted to set up your IAM role if it hasn't been done before.

✓ Maintain "advanced settings" as your default.

✓ Pick "Next" and review. Now create your function.

✓ Set up your event source. (In the Lambda function tab select "Event Source").

✓ Tap on "Add event source."

✓ Pick type as "Alexa Skill Test."

✓ Copy the ARN for your Lambda function. This will be needed for establishing the skill in the developer portal.

Setting up the skill in the Developer Portal

✓ Go to the developer portal account and migrate to Apps & services/Alexa/Alexa Skills set.

✓ Here your skill will be defined and managed.

✓ Choose "select a new skill" and add your name/invocation name.

✓ Choose "save" and "next."

✓ Define your skills interaction model.

✓ Copy and paste the following Intent schema:

{

```json
"intents": [
  {
    "intent": "AnswerIntent",
    "slots": [
      {
        "name": "Answer",
        "type": "LIST_OF_ANSWERS"
      }
    ]
  },

  {
    "intent": "AnswerOnlyIntent",
    "slots": [
      {
        "name": "Answer",
        "type": "LIST_OF_ANSWERS"
      }
    ]
  },
```

```json
    {
      "intent": "DontKnowIntent"
    },
    {
      "intent": "AMAZON.StartOverIntent"
    },
    {
      "intent": "AMAZON.RepeatIntent"
    },
    {
      "intent": "AMAZON.HelpIntent"
    },
    {
      "intent": "AMAZON.YesIntent"
    },
    {
      "intent": "AMAZON.NoIntent"
    },
    {
```

```
        "intent": "AMAZON.StopIntent"

    },

    {

        "intent": "AMAZON.CancelIntent"

    }

  ]

}
```

Now insert Slot type

Add the expressions. Copy and Paste these:

AnswerIntent the answer is {Answer}

AnswerIntent my answer is {Answer}

AnswerIntent is it {Answer}

AnswerIntent {Answer} is my answer

AnswerOnlyIntent {Answer}

AMAZON.StartOverIntent start game

AMAZON.StartOverIntent new game

AMAZON.StartOverIntent start

AMAZON.StartOverIntent start new game

DontKnowIntent I don't know

DontKnowIntent doesn't know

DontKnowIntent skip

DontKnowIntent I don't know that

DontKnowIntent who knows

DontKnowIntent I don't know this question

DontKnowIntent I don't know that one

DontKnowIntent dunno

Choose save, and you should now see the model being formed.

Hit "next."

Go to your ARN endpoint from your Lambda function, tap "No" for account linking and tap "next."

Ready to test

In your test tab enter an expression in the service simulator tab.

In this example we called the skill "reindeer games." This invocation name was set up in the skill information line previously in step#2.

Type in "open reindeer games" and select "Ask".

View the formatted JSON request from Alexa Service and the response coming back.

Look for your skill to be enabled in the Alexa Companion app (Your Echo device needs to be online and logged in with the same account as your developer account) and you should be able to ask Alexa to launch your skill.

It's Yours

Edit the skill information to show your trivia game:

New name

Creative invocation name

Good Icon

Leave everything else alone in the developer portal for now

Log into your AWS console and alter the Trivia Game Function you already generated. We are going to insert your new trivia game questions and answers.

We have edited our code in-line so edit your questions and answers so JSON will show your trivia game.

✓A few Ideas

Look and see that the format is for one question and four answers for each question. The first answer is the right answer. The script logic will randomize the questions and answers.

Go back to the Developer portal/skill for a moment. Paste in your "Skill Information" in the developer portal/skill in the Lambda script.

Head over to the AWS Lambda Function, find the ID application section and copy that application ID into the section indicated. Save It!

Remove any reindeer game questions. Start with 20 questions then upgrade to 100 questions as this will keep user's attention. Save and note we test in the Developer Portal, not the Lambda Function (AWS).

Now we will test/edit our skill back in the developer portal. After we are done here, we can have our skill-certified.

Migrate into your skills test tab and make a few expressions. We want to make sure everything is working well with the new questions and answers. Go ahead and test with your Alexa enabled device. We want to be sure all the words form correctly. You may have to repair a few words that sound wrong. Did you add your Application ID?

Critical:

The certification team will run every question and intent on an Echo device to make sure all is well. Do this ahead of time so you will pass the certification. Fix any question or answer that doesn't sound correct. If not, do you need to change any that sound wrong, so they are correct?

Choose the description tab next:

Pick some attractive description words to lure users to your game. They will appear in the Companion apps list of new skills available. Make sure you have the rights to any icons you load. You will need 108x108px and 512x512px images. If the certification teams have any doubts about the sizes, you will be failed.

Choose to save for certification:

In your publishing section choose "No" for spending money and collecting personal information. Privacy and terms URLs are your choices.

In your testing data, you are using the Trivia Game framework.

You may receive e-mails from the team on how to improve your skill. You can update your skills anytime.

How to Use IFTTT and Alexa to Find A Misplaced Phone

IFTTT adds much functionality to the Echo device. By visiting the Alexa IFTTT channel, you can discover so much that you can accomplish and automate with Alexa and your Echo.

Setting IFTTT recipes for your Echo and for use with Alexa is straightforward, as we have seen. One of the recipes that may come in handy and that you may want to set up is 'The Find My Phone'

As indicated earlier, to set up recipes for your Echo, you need an IFTTT account, if you don't have one, you should grab one now.

Once you have that in check, you want to browse for the recipe you want. In this case, on the search bar, we want to search for "Trigger find my Phone" Once you select this recipe, you'll need to connect the phone channel. This means providing your mobile phone number in the browser pop up (at the time of writing this, only US based numbers are compatible with the phone feature).

"Alexa, trigger find my phone"

Notes: Just say "Alexa, trigger find my phone" and this Recipe will call your phone.

Connect this Channel first

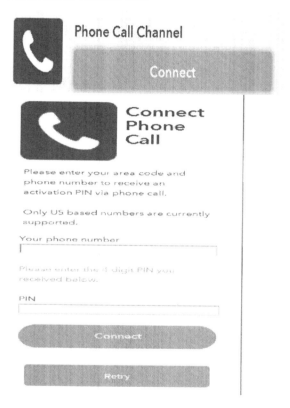

Once you enter an acceptable phone number, Amazon will instantaneously call you and provide you with a four-digit pin. Pay attention to the pin and write it down to avoid re-doing this step. Once you've verified everything, the recipe is ready for use and all you have to do is trigger it by saying "Alexa, trigger find my phone"

your phone should commence ringing in a few seconds i.e. if it is not muted or on vibrate only.

How to Create Additional, Personal Commands for Your Echo Device

Although the Amazon echo is a smart speaker, and a personal assistant, it is primarily a voice command device programmed to listen to commands and carry out these commands.

As we saw earlier, Alexa is at the heart and soul of the Echo. Without the smartness of Alexa, the Echo would just be another smart speaker.

In its out-of-the-box version, although Alexa is extremely smart, she does not come pre-equipped with a wide array of commands. What separates Alexa from other personal assistants such as the Cortana or Siri, is Alexa's adaptability. With the former two, getting the assistant to answer to commands is often a struggle especially if you talk too fast, are not a native English speaker, or if your enunciation is heavily accentuated. The echo is different. With voice training, unlike Cortana or Siri, Alexa can adapt to your speech patterns, accent, and way of speaking. In fact, Amazon suggests that once you get the Echo, speak to it not in a slow way, but in a normal way.

This is perhaps why more than anything, you have to voice train the echo to your voice and utterances

Amazon touts the Echo as the smartest, most intuitive voice command assistant in the world. The echo does not disappoint. By offering smart homes and gear support, and featuring third party integration, Alexa does possess the ability to become the most advanced voice command system in the world. With its adaptability to devices such as the WeMO, Belkin's Philips Hue, and some security systems, Alexa has found many uses around the home and office. All this is possible courtesy of the Echo's IFTTT ability.

IFTTT is a revolutionary way through which you can automate digital tasks such as reading and forwarding emails, digital calendars such as Google calendar, automated shopping, etc. IFTTT gives you the ability to create recipes or digital commands.

The IFTTT capability in Echo is perhaps the most profound and exciting thing about the echo. IFTTT opens up Echo usage to smart services and devices and makes the Echo the most adaptable voice command system in the world today.

Understanding IFTTT and How You Can Use It to Create Personal Commands for Your Echo

IFTTT is an automation, multiplatform service that gives you the ability to create commands, known as recipes, which connect two services that trigger an automatic action or response. IFTTT has found many uses in society. For example, you can use IFTTT recipes to forward starred emails into Evernote.

IFTTT stands for 'if this then that' which in simple terms means if this (if this happens), then that (then that should happen). Like everything else synonymous with the Echo, creating your own commands or recipes is relatively easy.

How to Create Personal Echo Commands

To create new echo commands, you need to setup your echo and ensure it's connected to your home network. We have already covered this step; if you haven't setup your Echo yet, do so now.

After you're all setup, the next thing you want to do is activate the Alexa IFTTT channel. To accomplish this, head over to the IFTTT website and sign up or in if you already have an account.

Once you sign in or sign up (sign up is free), on the upper right hand corner, you shall see a "Channels" option. Click on this and scroll down to find the Amazon Alexa Channel. Activation of the channel is a breeze. Simply click on the "connect" option; securely enter your Amazon credentials for integration authorization.

Once you authorize, you can immediately start creating recipes. You can do this by clicking 'my recipes' from the IFTTT homepage then clicking on the highly, visible "Create a Recipe" button.

Designing an IFTTT recipe is easy. You need to create an 'if' trigger and a 'then' trigger or action. This is the bane of using personal commands with your Echo device. In our case, since our Echo is the trigger, our aim is to ensure that each time we give Alexa a specific personally curated command; it triggers a specific action or response.

On the IFTTT Alexa channel, click on the blue 'this' to get rolling. This will prompt IFTTT to bring up all its channels; click on Amazon Alexa. Since we have already gone through the activation phase, you should not encounter an activation dialog here. In case you do, go through the activation or authorization step.

From there, you shall see a list of triggers. There are many options available here especially since Amazon opened up Echo development to third party developers. However, since our aim is to create specific verbal commands, you want to select the "Say a Specific Phrase" once you select this, IFTTT will prompt you for the phrase you want to use.

When creating a phrase:

1: Note that, because Alexa primarily responds to her wake word, and a trigger that tells her to listen out for a custom IFTTT phrase, your IFTTT command must start with the wake word 'Alexa' (if you haven't changed the wake word to something else) and trigger ("Alexa Trigger") followed by your custom phrase.

2: When typing your custom phrase, you should only do so in lowercase and avoid punctuations.

For our example, we shall stick to 'my recipe" as the trigger and finish by choosing the 'create trigger' option. This means every time we say, "Alexa, trigger my recipe" our recipe will fire up. This takes care of the 'if' part of the equation. We next need to calibrate the 'then' part.

The action you want Alexa to carry out can range from social media integration, web tools such as email integration, and smart devices control.

In our case, we shall work towards creating a new command to control a smart device: **The Nest Learning Thermostat.** The Nest Learning Thermostat does not feature a custom-built Echo integration. Thus, creating a new IFTTT recipe creates a bridge between this type of thermostat and your Echo device or other smart products.

In our instance, if we look at the Nest IFTTT channel, we have various options available. In the Nest channel, Alexa can set the Thermostat heat to a specific temperature, trigger the circulation of fans for a specific period such as 15 minutes, or adjust between air conditioning and automated heat.

if You say "Alexa trigger my recipe" **then** Turn on Hallway Thermostat fan for 15 minutes

Recipe Title

If You say "Alexa trigger my recipe", then turn on Hallway Thermostat fan for 15 minutes

Receive notifications when this Recipe runs

Create Recipe

From here, what you do will vary on your 'that' calibration. In this instance, when we trigger our recipe, we want Alexa to turn on the Thermostat fans for 15 minutes. In this case, all we need to do is select "turn on fans for 15 minutes" as our action. Now, as indicated earlier, what you do for the action will largely depend on your 'that' settings and the channel you choose for your action.

Logically, some 'then' channels will have more actions than others will. What you should note is that, in almost all of these channels, creating a command for your Echo should be as easy as navigating through a dropdown, itemized lists.

After we're done choosing our action, all we need to do know is click "Create Action" and IFTTT will offer an end version of your recipe. If everything seems in order, create the recipe and you're done: you've just created a new voice command for your Echo.

The most amazing thing about the Echo and its integration with IFTTT is that as an Amazon Echo user, you have limitless possibilities when it comes to creating new commands for Alexa to follow. Creating new commands for Alexa is easy and fun.

Experiment with many phrases and triggers to customize your Echo to your exact specification, as well as make the echo work for you.

Amazon Echo Troubleshooting

As a new technological device, it is likely that you may feel completely stranded should something appear to be wrong with your Amazon Echo. Most of the issues that could arise are not because there is something that is technically amiss with the device; rather, it may be something that you do not understand how to do which is in turn affecting your device's functionality. Here are some things that you can easily deal with should they arise.

The Solid Orange Light

For the most part, the light ring at the top of your device will be shades of dark and light blue as it responds to you. Should there be changes in color, particularly the ring changing to write or orange, it means that there may be issues with your Wi-Fi connection. A light that is solid orange indicates that the Amazon Echo has not yet connected to the Wi-Fi network or the cloud.

To resolve this issue, you need to try to reconnect to your Wi-Fi network. This will require you to use your Alexa app, where you will see the option to Rescan. Choose that option for a quick solution.

Broken Communication

Sometimes, you may speak to Alexa and she does not understand what you are trying to say. Should this occur, there are several things you could attempt. To begin with, reduce the speed of your speech, and try to pronounce your words more clearly. You could also cut out all the noise in the background. If you still have a problem, take some time to complete voice training with Alexa, so that she is able to better comprehend what you are trying to communicate.

No Bluetooth Connection

Are you attempting to play music from your mobile device using Alexa and it is just not working, as you would like? The issue may be in your Bluetooth connection. When the Bluetooth has been switched on from your device, simply command Alexa to pair with it, by saying 'Alexa pair.' You will be able to choose your Amazon Echo to pair with from the list that appears on your mobile device.

Get Help

Since you are dealing with a machine, you might have believed that getting the help you need can be a challenge, especially when you ask Alexa a question about her operations, which she is unable to answer for you. Luckily, many customer care representatives are available and ready to respond to any queries that you may have about using your Amazon Echo and getting friendly with Alexa. To get in touch with them, you need to use your web browser and visit http://echo.amaon.com/#help/call. Once you are there, type your number into the box and you will receive a call from someone who can assist you. You will find that they are highly familiar with the way that the Amazon Echo works and can give you the help that you need.

Privacy Concerns

Every instruction or command that you give to the Amazon Echo is stored in a cloud by Amazon. This is so that it is possible for Alexa to offer you better service, as the pool of information will clarify your common commands, as well as information that you access often. Some people may not be comfortable knowing that their information is somewhere in a cloud, and therefore, require more privacy. This is possible, as by accessing the Amazon Echo site, you can choose to delete some recordings individually, or if you want, you can delete all the recordings that are in the cloud from your Echo.

Conclusion

Amazon Echo is definitely more than just a speaker; it can entertain you, provide you with any information on tap, execute commands you give to it, and help you enjoy some fun as you use it. It is an amazing and a great device to have at home if you want to enjoy its convenience and the services its software has to offer.

In summary, some of its pros are:

Good Audio

Amazing Design

Endless Information

Accurate Voice Recognition

Great Sound Quality

Fun to Use

It is quite affordable; only retailing at $199.00 and for this, you get so much convenience you can never enjoy from any device.

The only problem that has been noted with the Echo is that it lacks a built-in battery, which is no problem at all since it can be used from any other room other than where it is. As long as it is connected to a Wi-Fi network, you can give it commands from any direction or room in the house.

So much more should be expected from the Amazon Echo as Amazon plans to update more and more features as it receives feedback from Echo users. As more features are added to it, you will get to enjoy more services, which is just amazing.

This device is becoming a necessity in any household. It is not just an entertainment device but also a helper whenever you are working at home. It can help you with simple math calculations, provide you with any information you need, help you with your homework or projects that could need information from Wikipedia, help you perform simple duties at home like turning on the oven, AC lights, and so many other appliances that you have connected to Echo. It is an easier means to communicate to different family members at the same time when they are in different locations in the house.

All this and much more are possible if you have the Amazon Echo. So, start shopping now and enjoy its use.